ALL FOR A SHILLING A DAY

Also by Donald Featherstone and available in the NEL series:

MACDONALD OF THE 42ND
THE BOWMEN OF ENGLAND
AT THEM WITH THE BAYONET

All for a Shilling a Day

Donald Featherstone

NEW ENGLISH LIBRARY
TIMES MIRROR

First published in Great Britain by Jarrolds Publishers (London) Ltd., 1966

*

FIRST NEL PAPERBACK EDITION AUGUST 1973
Reprinted January 1974

*

NEL Books are published by
New English Library Limited from Barnard's Inn, Holborn, London, E.C.1.
Made and printed in Great Britain by Hunt Barnard Printing Ltd., Aylesbury, Bucks.

450015858

Contents

Introduction

This is the dramatised but authentic story of two years in the life of a famous regiment of the British Army. It is not a history of the 16th, the Queen's Lancers, but the existence of the men of that regiment from the very day that some of them enlisted until they either survived or succumbed to injuries received in battle; or recovered in spite of the primitive battlefield surgery of the day.

One hundred and twenty years ago, on the 28th of January 1846, a relatively small battle was fought at Aliwal in the Punjab of India. It was not a particularly important battle in that it did not make or break an empire, although it did much to bring to a rapid and successful conclusion the first Sikh War. This was a campaign in which an out-gunned and outnumbered British Army 'saved' India by defeating the martial Sikhs, toughest of all the enemies they encountered in that country. The commander of the British force who won the battle was an elderly but dashing veteran of the Peninsular Wars, Sir Harry Smith, a colourful figure who rivals any hero of fiction. His victory at Aliwal had claims to fame. It was considered by military experts to be almost unique as 'the battle without a mistake'. Sir Harry in his report wrote: '. . . my fight at Aliwal was a little sweeping second edition of Salamanca – a stand-up gentleman-like battle, a mixing of all arms and laying on, carrying everything before by weight of attack and combination, all hands at work from one end of the field to the other.'

The battle also featured that most spine-tingling of all military occurrences – a full-scale cavalry charge. It was performed by the 16th, the Queen's Lancers, who lost more than a quarter of their strength in repeatedly breaking through formed squares of highly trained infantry – a rare feat in cavalry annals. Long since forgotten except by the military historian, this charge was justly acclaimed by all at the time and served as a classic example until overshadowed by the heavy and light brigades at Balaclava, eight years later.

This is the story of a typical British Cavalry regiment during the early part of Queen Victoria's long reign. The 16th, the Queen's Lancers, were a regiment later to be proud of the fact that its survivors of the battle of Aliwal paraded on the following day with lance pennons so encrusted with dried blood that they appeared to be starched and crimped, leading to a regimental tradition from then on that the 16th Lancers should always have crimped lance pennons. The regiment was no different from any other cavalry regiment of its day. It contained aristocrats, men of high birth who were arrogant and disdainful but outstandingly courageous; men who held the power of life and death over their underlings, the low-born, the illiterate, the scorned. But these men were also very brave, partly because they were rigidly and brutally disciplined to conform to the often tactically ridiculous orders given them by their superiors and partly because they were truly professional fighting men. There is a high example to be found in the touchingly simple bravery of these coarse, uneducated men who joined the Army as a last resort because they were hungry, cold, unemployed and often unemployable; scorned by the society that made them what they were. By today's standards these men were treated with stark brutality. This might serve to give a derogatory impression of the 16th Lancers and the British Army, but it must be remembered that the treatment that they received and their rights were those considered reasonable in the period in which they lived. Just before the time of the events recorded in this book the slaves were freed with a great show of indignation, but soldiers continued to be flogged until 1881.

English literature gives sparse treatment to the British soldier, with the possible exception of Shakespeare's *King Henry V* or Kipling's *Barrack Room Ballads* or *Soldiers Three*. Few writers have told how the ordinary soldier lived, although his victories were described long after his bones had salted the plains of India, the roads of Spain or the sands of the Sudan. The men of Cromwell, Marlborough, Wolfe and Wellington seem to have vanished unrecorded as though they never existed as human beings; no one knows very much of how they talked in barracks or on the night before a battle or what they thought of their officers or of each other. This is sad, because they were men worthy of being remembered, men whose deeds were capable of influencing the heedless society for whom they were winning empires. It has been said that Kipling '. . . moulded a whole generation of young Englishmen who rose up in their thousands in 1914 and sacrificed themselves in the image that he had created'. It is doubtful if any other writer can claim to have done as much.

Every name mentioned in this book is that of a man who actually lived and served in the 16th, the Queen's Lancers, through these events and in this period. Some of the related occurrences may not feature these actual men or this regiment, but, nevertheless, they are completely authentic and all took place at that period to other soldiers serving in other regiments.

The less civilised man has an advantage in war, a natural advantage in that his wants are simple and that his life is normally one of hardship and frugality, being rated comparatively lightly because it is so laborious. But standards change and the toughness of the ancients always seems greater than that of the present generation. Gibbon, writing 150 years or more ago, said of the Roman legionary that the weight he carried would 'oppress the delicacy of the modern soldier'. When one recalls that Gibbon was writing of the soldiers of his day, the men who fought at Minden and who were shortly to fight in the Peninsular, one would certainly hesitate to class them as delicate! The man who wore the British red coat did not win every battle in which he fought but he was never once disgraced; he was unnoticed and unheralded and he was held in contempt by the people for whom he fought and died, because he was a man apart from the rest of the community.

D.F.F.

1

The Recruits

The Recruiting Sergeant was tall and well built; his big chest filled out the scarlet, double-breasted coat bearing two rows of glittering buttons, gold epaulettes, loops and tassels. His well-fed florid face proudly wore expansive and carefully trimmed moustaches curling on to both cheeks. On his head a pillbox forage cap from which fluttered coloured ribbons. He was made to look even taller by long, straddling legs in tight, blue overalls, down the sides of which ran double gold stripes, strapped beneath gleaming boots with musically jingling spurs.

The recruits were of poor physique, their clothes were crumpled and creased, as though they had been slept in. All were dirty and unshaven, as they had had no opportunity of washing since the previous day. Two of the men had the flat, pinched faces of Irishmen – faces becoming increasingly familiar as the potato famine drove them from the squalid cabins in their own starving country.[1] Pathetically trying to retain a measure of assumed social dignity, one of the recruits stood on his own a few paces away. He wore clothes a little less ragged and of better style than his companions and he had been classified by the Recruiting Sergeant as a clerk or shop assistant who had unwisely dipped into the petty-cash box. The fourth recruit was older than the others; he had been brought from the cells after being before the Justice of the Peace on charges of begging and vagrancy. Having been given the option of going to prison or joining the Army, he had decided upon the latter.[2]

They were all hungry and bewildered so that they started violently when a clipped roar filled the air:

'Come on, now! Let's be having you!'

The Recruiting Sergeant faced them, stiffly erect, head thrust slightly forward, eyes bulging; the fingers of his left hand stretched straining down the seam of his overalls, his right hand clutched the short cane that was tucked under his arm. Moving towards them, he pushed and bustled the shuffling group into a rough line; he then thrust a Testament into each uncomprehending hand. Crashingly, he saluted the Magistrate who had entered the room:

'All present and correct, Your Worship!'

His Worship nodded absently, staring curiously through his old-fashioned spectacles at the bedraggled men paraded in front of him. He held up his hand – his voice was old and dry.

'Now, listen to me, you men! All of you here do make Oath that you will be faithful and bear true allegiance to Her Majesty, her Heirs and Successors, Crown and Dignity against all enemies. . . . Observe and obey all orders of Her Majesty . . . of all the Generals and Officers set over me . . . So Help You, God! Now, kiss the Book. Take them away, Sergeant.'

The tired, cracked voice died away. The recruits were pushed out of the dust-smelling police court and shepherded through side streets back to the recruiting office. In a bare and dingy room they were roughly ordered to strip; the unaccustomed mass-nakedness produced an odd self-consciousness. In a very short time they had all been sounded, measured and weighed by an impassive doctor; answered questions put to them by a lean, wizened Corporal who scribbled their answers on to official-looking printed forms. During this ceremony the Recruiting Sergeant impatiently hovered around, now completely lacking the chaffing geniality of an hour past. Finally, everyone went out, locking the door behind them, and left the recruits to hang around aimlessly in the featureless room for two hours or more.

Suddenly and noisily the door was opened and the Corporal slid around it. He drew himself up in a pale imitation of the manner of the Recruiting Sergeant and roared at them:

'Come on, now! Get fell in outside! I'm here to escort yer to Hounslow Barracks an' heaven help anyone o' yer who tries to make a break for it!'

He surveyed them steadily, his glance sliding slyly from one side of the room to the other; the crafty, lined face broke into a blackened-toothed grin. Pushing his hand into the depths of his tunic he brought out a bottle; he waved it at them:

'Come on now, me lucky lads! Who says a penn'orth o' gin?'

Tears started in their eyes at this unexpected friendly gesture; they took generous swigs from the bottle until it was empty; the Corporal wiped his mouth with the back of his hand. He hurried them outside and formed them up in the road; he gave a quick word of command and they trudged off. The Corporal marched by himself on the pavement, trying to create the impression that he was in no way connected with the shambling quartet in the gutter.

Civilian passers-by moved to avoid them and gazed with unfriendly eyes; in the minds of these ordinary God-fearing citizens there was no such thing as a 'good soldier'. For a member of one's family 'to go for a soldier' was a crowning disgrace – to join the Army was as good as being consigned to moral ruin.[3]

At Paddington Station the teeming clamour and fearsome blasts of released steam from the spidery-wheeled locomotives with their gaily coloured boilers seemed to betoken their transmigration from the old world they knew to the unknown one in front of them. The recruits forgot their hunger under the spell of this five-year-old novelty that took them bumping and rattling amid showers of cinders in open third-class trucks. London soon lay behind them, dull roofs packed under the far-reaching smoke mists gave way to brick viaducts and then market gardens, fields and clusters of cottages.

The drab little station at which their journey ended stood dismally alone at the end of a branch line – they found out later that its patrolled exclusiveness was designed as a deterrent to the potential deserter. They tumbled stiffly out on to the platform under the critical eye of a smart Sergeant in the lancer's uniform they were soon to know so well. Roughly but not unkindly he fell them in, signed for their bodies and took over from the Corporal, who gave them a raucous farewell. At the Sergeant's word of command they gathered themselves up and marched in shambling fashion out of the station yard.

Even in their hunger-inspired apathy they were still able to raise enough curiosity to gaze around them at the geometrically laid-out community through which they were marching. It was a half rural, half urban oasis, built only a few years before, consisting of gaunt rectangular barrack buildings of bright red brick surrounded by a small town of mean grey houses. Lacking the time to mellow and weather, the place had a raw look[4] emphasised by the bleak gorse-grown heath in which it had been set down. There was a proliferation of ever-open beer-shops, with appropriate titles such as 'The Gallant Duke', 'The Gay Hussar' and 'The Waterloo Arms'.[5]

Their unseeing eyes failed to comprehend the many ominous signs of the nature of existence in this community – where Time was of little consequence and was made known by trumpet notes when required so that no one cared because all four faces of the clock in the angular tower showed different times to their neighbours. Large black-and-white notices warned those who could read that 'OTHER RANKS ARE FORBIDDEN TO USE THE PAVEMENTS' and that 'THIS ROAD IS OUT OF BOUNDS TO OTHER RANKS' – the illiterate soon painfully discovered the meanings of such signs. There was an overlay of quiet broken only by sounds of a military nature, the blare of trumpets, the clatter of marching feet and the harsh cry of orders. The clamour and bustle of London's streets was replaced by an almost foreboding air of passive obedience that spawned sullen alertness whilst it thrust aside mirth and gaiety.

Short as the march was from the station to the barracks, the military hush had time to bring unease to the recruits; even the regulation noises that broke the disciplined quiet caused them to start nervously. They heard unseen and regulated feet crunch in complicated manoeuvres to the clipped shouts of drill instructors; the rhythmic trample of horses' hooves from the far side of a high wall caused them to crane their necks. Then their ears were suddenly assailed by the heavy metallic rumble of the iron-shod wheels of guns and limbers with an accompaniment of the rattle and jingle of the gun-team's harness.

Turning a corner, they came upon the high iron gates of the barracks. All eyes turned to the splendidly – nay, gloriously – attired sentry who stood stiffly in front of the brick pillar; without turning his head the sentry disdainfully glanced back at them from the corners of his eyes. They marched past him, past the barred windows of the guardroom and skirted the bare windswept square framed by the façade and tower of the barrack buildings. The rapped order from their Sergeant bewildered them as much as his sudden convulsive stiffening of the head and body as he saluted to his right. The target of his respect was a small lawn enclosed by spiked chains and white-painted posts; from the middle of the clipped grass rose a white flagpole from which hung the regimental colours of the 16th, the Queen's Lancers.

They were bustled down a side alley and handed over to a haughty Corporal, who demanded their names and then flew into a rage at the different pronunciations offered by the recruits and their wild ideas of spelling. He seemed particularly put out by the luckless Irish lads and forecast the most lurid fates for them . . . 'when yer Troop S'arn't gits at'cher!' He turned disgustedly from them and hurried back into the building, leaving them confused and ignored until their collective gaze lit upon a startling figure bearing down on them.

Very tall and very thin, bowed legs seemingly poured into skin-tight overalls surmounted by a uniform of immaculate and colourful perfection, the new arrival stalked towards them in an aura of menace. Like rabbits, before a snake, the recruits found awed fascination in the jerky, even steps that seemed to have been borrowed from a jointed marionette. Convulsively, the steps abruptly ceased as the figure crashed into wooden-soldier rigidity; the shabby quartet gazed at him in petrified stupefaction. Head thrust forward, he glared back at them, eyes standing out in the lean, bronzed and lined face with its embellishment of whiskers curling down from the brim of his peaked forage cap. Apparently wishing to inspect them even more closely, he jerked into slow, even-paced steps until he had twice circled them to the tune of the regular clinking of spurs as he jauntily threw out his brilliantly polished boots. Finally, he crashed once again into the wooden-soldier position and assumed the attitude of pent-up anger that they were soon to recognise as the military precursor of a terrifying tirade.

'In all my days as a so'jer . . . an' I've bin Regimental S'arn't-Major o' the 16th, the Queen's Lancers, fer fourteen year . . . I have never . . . no never . . . seen a filthier, dirtier, unso'jerlike scum than wot's standing in front of me right now!'

He drew a deep breath, inflating his braid-bestrewn chest, glared at each of them in turn, and his hoarse, cracked roar assaulted them again:

'Now, lissen to me . . . lissen very very carefully . . . becos I'm warning you . . . all o' you . . . my little eyes will be on you night an' day . . . there won't be a moment when S'arn't-Major McQueen won't know wot you're up to!'

The voice took on a quieter, semi-wheedling note:

'So, let's unnerstand each other right from the start, shall we?'

The Regimental Sergeant-Major cocked his bullet-shaped head to one side questioningly, jerked it back to the centre and opened his whiskered mouth wide. What emerged was probably the loudest human voice that any of the recruits had ever heard in their lives:

'Becos if you don't . . . I'll have your guts for garters . . . that I swear!'

As though to confirm his unspoken claim of having eyes in the back of his head, the R.S.M. swung round and presented his stiff back to them. His right arm flashed up in salute and his body remained in ramrod position for perhaps five seconds before the hand swooped downwards to his side.

Along the gravelled path strode a tall middle-aged man even more gloriously dressed than the Sergeant-Major. He acknowledged the salute with a flick of his glove and stood looking at the strangely contrasting group of ex-civilians. In a bored, quiet monotone the officer addressed them:

'You are new men here and you will soon be wearing red. Red is the Army colour, red is the colour of the Queen's liveries, and you will be private troopers of the 16th, the Queen's Lancers – known as the Red Lancers because we are the only lancer regiment to still wear a red jacket.'

He paused, as though trying to recall his lines, although he had rendered this speech often enough. Finding inspiration in the sky above the nearest recruit's head, he continued:

'A regiment is a little society, a little club, of soldiers; it has a life of its own which goes on not only from year to year but from century to century. Men like you . . . just like you . . . come and go; they end their term of service, or are killed in battle or die of disease, but recruits always come in and learn from the older soldiers how to keep up the good name of the regiment.'

Pausing again, he paced up and down in front of them, glaring at them sideways from half-closed eyes.

'Er . . . men like you come and go, but the regiment lives on, its battle honours are embroidered on our saddle-cloths to remind us of the brave deeds done by those who came before us.'

He stopped pacing, stood motionless for a moment; gazed at the open-mouthed bunch of recruits. He knew that few if any of them had understood more than an odd word here and there of his routine speech. His gaze transferred to the Sergeant-Major:

'You'll turn 'em into what I want, Sergeant-Major, you always do. You know, I've always said that for butcher's work, uneducated blackguards led by gentlemen are the most efficient!'

The Sergeant-Major stiffened:

'Yessir! Just as you say, sir!'[6]

2

Training Begins

Struggling back to consciousness, the recruits momentarily found it difficult to realise where they were. There was a puzzling background of noise – doors banging, voices shouting, feet clattering and, riding high over it all, the piercing note of a trumpet repeating its lilting air. The climb back to life was further hindered by the foul atmosphere of the barrack-room – a combination of perspiring human bodies, insufficiently aired clothes, the aroma of generations of steaming meals blending with the penetrating, acrid reek from the stables below. Shatteringly, a hoarse roar battered at their drowsy senses:

'Come on! Let's be havin' yer! Six o'clock an' yer still snoring! The Colonel's compliments and will you get up or do you want him to come and drag you out by the scruff of the neck? Get up, get up! Don't you hear me or won't you hear me? Are you deaf or are you in a trance? Get out of those stinking pits and have a wash . . . go on, the lot o' you . . . wash your filthy selves . . . then come back and clean up the room. Quick's the word!'

Without waiting to see the effect of his words, the brisk Sergeant vanished, leaving the bemused recruits sitting on the edges of their beds, feet on the ground. Their surroundings hardly encouraged wakefulness; it might have been more merciful if they could have slept it all off as a bad dream.

'C' Troop's barrack-room was a low-roofed loft over the stables, reached by an outside flight of wooden stairs. It consisted of nothing but the sleeping chamber, there were no ablution rooms or rooms in which to eat. Sanitary arrangements were of the crudest: a pair of large urine tubs stood in the middle of the room and added to the night-time stench – they were hurriedly washed out each morning to serve as washbasins. The men washed at a single pump in the yard below, scrambling around in the muddy slush that spread for yards around the ever-dripping pump. Water flew on all sides as the forty men all tried to wash at the same time; shirts and trousers became sodden and had to dry 'on the body'. In winter this exodus from the fetid and oppressive atmosphere of the barrack-room into the bitter cold was the cause of a great many bronchial and tubercular illnesses.

On the previous night the recruits had been given two dirty, ragged brown blankets and the promise of a bolster . . . 'when there were some to spare'. They slept in their shirts, with their boots and rolled-up clothes under their heads for pillows; beneath them canvas palliasse covers filled with straw from the stables rested on the iron slats of the cot; there was a bare six inches between each pair of the forty beds.[1]

Each of the four corners of the low-roofed room were screened by a bedraggled, holed blanket that hung unevenly on a piece of rope. Behind these screens the married men of the troop carried on their matrimonial life and brought up their children from tender infancy.[2]

Under the direction of the older soldiers the recruits took their part in cleaning and tidying the room. They lined their beds up on each other, folded their blankets meticulously to the same squared shape as their neighbour's and stowed away out of sight their few personal belongings. Breakfast was eaten standing up or perched uncomfortably on the end of the bed so as not to disturb its neat appearance. It consisted of an unappetising lump of hard, greyish barrack-baked bread with a mug of coarse tea.[3]

The recruits stood around forlornly, bemused by the bustle of the remainder of the troop preparing for the day's first parade – signalled by the shrill blare of a trumpet. The men were galvanised into a state of feverish activity, madly funnelling towards the top of the wooden staircase that led down to the yard below. As the last of them vanished he urgently beckoned them to follow; they clattered down a few yards behind the older soldiers, uniform in their fatigue dress. In the yard the men formed up in regular lines; the recruits stared helplessly at each other and finally formed up at one end in a pathetic undisciplined bunch.

The Troop Sergeant called the troop to order briskly, brought them up to attention and then inspected them minutely. A number of the men had their names taken for one infringement or another and the recruits tremblingly awaited the three-striped awesome figure to reach them. However, he halted when he came to the last of the uniformed men; he fixed the confused recruits with a long, keen glare and, without moving his eyes from them, called up the Troop Corporal.

'C'pl . . . take this lot to the Q.M.'s stores.'

'S'ar'nt!'

The Sergeant marched off the remainder of the troop, leaving the Corporal slowly circling the four men as though appalled and disgusted by what he saw. After a brief but to the point diatribe, he marched them off through the lines, past tumbledown buildings and huts until they reached a barred-windowed shed that bore the notice 'Quartermaster's Stores'. They were shepherded into the dim, camphor-smelling cavern that consisted of row upon row of floor-to-ceiling racks, each compartment being stuffed with clothing and equipment. There were recognisable items in the nearest racks – folded tunics and trousers; wellington boots; round boxes that they soon discovered contained tall lance-caps and other mysterious recesses that stretched into the twilight horizon at the rear of the hut.

Each man in turn went up to the wooden, blanket-covered counter behind which sat a fat Quartermaster-Sergeant sucking a stub of pencil. He laboriously filled in their names at the top of a form, at the same time casually mentioning that the various items of clothing and equipment he was about to issue would cost them just about the exact amount of the cash bounty they had been promised on enlistment.

The Q.M.'s orderly began a fast-moving, swift-talking programme of transferring clothing and equipment from the shelves into their bewildered arms.

' 'Ere, catch 'old – this 'ere's yer lance-'at.'

They grasped a tall flat-topped hat with a cloth cover of blue; it had a gold-bullion rosette to hold the black cock's-tail feather that would droop sixteen inches in front when the cap was worn; the rosette had the 'VR' cypher embroidered on velvet. The gilt-rayed plate in front of the cap had the Queen's Arms and the gilt chin chain was fastened at the sides by a lion's head. Then followed a round forage cap, a scarlet jacket with blue facings and a slashed flap on the sleeves and two buttons at the back, two pairs of blue trousers, each with double stripes down the sides, one pair with gold and one with scarlet, a pair of white fatigue trousers, white gauntlet gloves, half-wellington boots, elegantly cut with pointed toes, curved steel spurs and the screws to fasten them into the heels. Then followed a puzzling collection of belts and straps, pouches and shabraques – there seemed no end to the burden piling up in their arms. And more was to follow: a stable jacket of white canvas, sets of harsh underclothing, three shirts and three pairs of socks, a razor, the mess-kit with knife, fork and spoon . . . a profusion of apparel far in excess of anything they had ever owned in their lives; they felt strangely rich and forgot the nagging rage of their forfeited bounty.

The recruits were told to try on each part of the uniform, their fumbling efforts to dress themselves being loftily supervised by the disdainful orderly. Their discarded, possibly verminous, civilian clothing he confiscated as it fell to the floor, swiftly rolling it up into lumpy bundles. The Quartermaster-Sergeant authorised his activities, repeating expressionlessly:

'It's a punishable offence for a so'jer to have civilian clothing.'

The orderly nodded his head after every repetition of the words; he would then turn to the confused recruit, bundle in his hand:

'You never had nothin' in them pockets, did yer?'

Before the newcomers could realise that they had just said goodbye to the few remaining coppers of their recruiting shilling, or perhaps a pocket-knife or some treasured memento of civilian days, the bundle had disappeared from view.

The four men were then paraded before the Quartermaster-Sergeant, who had waddled round from behind his counter; he attended closely to the more apparent misfits that caught his eye.

'Get this man a smaller cap . . . these boots are too small an' this one wants a larger tunic.'

'Please, sir . . . these boots pinch me toes.'

'This 'ere white jacket thing throttles me.'

The Quartermaster-Sergeant paid no attention whatsoever to their complaints; he stood back and looked them over.

'Quiet! This ain't Savile Row! You'll make 'em do or there'll be trouble! Now, Corp'l . . . march 'em out of my sight, the horrible men!'[4]

Arms full, and with straps dangling and dragging behind them, the laden party shambled back to the barrack-room. Dramatically, the air was filled with the plaintive and heart-searching sound of the assembled regimental trumpets playing the 16th Lancers' own elaborately harmonised variation of 'Stables'. The music swept over them like an emotional flood to affect even the dullest of them so that he felt his sense of confinement and humiliation flow away. In its place remained a secret reassurance that he had freed himself for ever from the drabness and poverty of the life he had left behind him.

Back in the barrack-room they were badgered, bullied and instructed into the correct method of stowing away their equipment. By the time they had completed it to his satisfaction the morning had passed and the trumpet sounded 'Dinner up!' The rest of the troop came clattering in and the famished men eagerly dragged out the board and trestles and set them up in the alley between the cots. The cookhouse orderlies of the day had long since rushed off to fetch the meal; back they came with great tins of boiled beef and blackened potatoes that gave off a far from appetising smell. The food was distributed and pushed down by the old soldiers, who begged for more of the greasy gravy or 'gyppo' – the flavour of which covered many of the sins of the food contractors.[5] This was to be the last meal of the day; from dinner-time until next morning there would be no more food issued – unless a man had the money to buy himself a supper he ate no more until the following day's breakfast.[6]

Together with half a dozen equally bemused recruits from other troops, they spent the afternoon on the square; their stiff ill-fitting fatigue dress rubbed raw their bare necks crudely cropped by the regimental barber; the hot summer sun burned down on them. The Drill Sergeant was a frightening man; ramrod straight, immaculate and polished, he was a despot who savoured the pleasure of words, using them unsparingly in a peculiarly impersonal manner that had the impact of a club.

'Now! Pay attention! Stand up smartly! Look straight to your front! Chin up! Shoulders back! Hands down the centre seam of the trousers . . . hollow your backs! Now! On the command . . . "Stand at haise!" . . . I want you to . . .'

At the end of the demonstration he brought them up to the old-fashioned 'Easy' – with hands clasped in front of them.

'Now! Lissen to me . . . pay attention! I'm not talking to amuse you but so that you will understand the spirit of the regiment . . . so just you lissen!'

The Drill Sergeant looked keenly at the oddly assorted bunch of recruits; his eyes travelled along their dull faces:

'A good soldier must have discipline – which means that he must learn his trade well. Discipline is teaching a man to do something which he would *not* do unless he had learned that it was the right, the proper and the most sensible thing to do under the circumstances. You learn discipline by having pride in yourselves, pride in your regiment . . . and . . . by fear of punishment. Discipline is saluting and smartness at your drill – saluting shows respect for an officer's uniform and his commission. Good drill makes you feel good and is the best and quickest way of doing the job. Discipline makes you learn by practice to do something without thinking so that it becomes natural when you are under fire. It was discipline that enabled the British line to defeat the French infantry column . . . and it was the British square that held off Napoleon's cavalry at Waterloo. So you are going to learn discipline if it kills you!"[7]

He stepped back; his body tensed, his hands stretched downwards as though reaching for something; his head craned forward; with the exception of his eyes flickering back and forward, he was rigid and motionless:

'Party! Wait for it . . . wait for it . . . that's only the 'cautionary word! Party! 'Shun!'

There was an appreciable difference in the crispness with which the recruits straightened their knees and slapped their hands back to trouser seams. Then followed an exhausting progression of marching back and forth over the sun-baked square. They were exhorted to swing their arms high; they were taught to turn and bring their heels together without catching their feet in their unfamiliar spurs; they painfully learned the elements of drill to the barked commands of the merciless Drill Sergeant.

When they had been going for about an hour they were brought up to the 'easy' position as a column of men on horses passed by them. They were picturesque as they sat straight in their saddles, their lances reaching high to the sky, pennants drooping limply in the still air. Sternly, the Drill Sergeant ordered them to look straight to their front:

'Don't get the idea . . . any of you . . . that you'll be doing that within a few days! It'll be a hell of a long time before any of you will be allowed within a mile of a horse! Before you can ride you've got to learn to *walk*! An' when I say "walk" I means *march* . . . marching like a so'jer! So, come on . . . let's get on with making so'jers out of you!'

3

Learning to be Lancers

In the months that followed, life was an unending progression of ceaseless foot-drill, dismounted sword exercises and meaningless fatigue parades accompanied by humiliation and degradation.[1] Upon the hard, foot-beaten surface of the square they formed and re-formed, quick marched, slow marched, wheeled and turned about until their heads spun and they went all ways at once when suddenly ordered to find their 'front'. Errors brought down upon their heads showers of invective and sarcasm, or punishments of varying types, according to the mood of the non-commissioned officer who happened to be badgering them at the time.

However bad this might have appeared to be, it was little in comparison to the sword exercises to which they eventually graduated. These exercises demanded exceptional strength of the arm to hold the heavy weapon straight at the 'front point', with arm extended and wrist turned – for long moments that seemed like hours, during which their instructor ruthlessly demanded that they held their positions. The fingers became numb and were unable to perform any longer; the sword would fall to the ground with a ringing clash.[2] This would transform their instructor into a demented, raving tyrant, and would earn the offender extra fatigues in the shape of two back-breaking hours carrying corn-sacks up a ladder to a loft over the forage stores.

The exhaustion and tedium of the endless drill, coupled with the scouring and cleaning of equipment, would not have been so demoralising had there been any relief in their scanty leisure hours. But they were left to get through their free time as best they might with only the little assistance offered by their meagre daily pay.[3]

As cavalrymen, they had a horse and saddlery to look after as well as themselves and their kit; they did not have many idle moments, and there were few relatively wholesome means of occupying them. Their free time, if not spent in the beer-shops, had to be passed in the stuffy and cramped barrackroom over the stables, where a man could scarcely squeeze in to reach the cot, his only seat. In the dark days the allowance of light was limited to two tallow-dips to every room of twelve men. Six or eight soldiers would huddle around a comrade, trying to hear him as he read aloud to them by the wretched illumination of one such dip.

Pay stoppages were made for articles of equipment, alleged damages to clothing or the barrack-room and for necessary cleaning materials such as soap, blacking and brick-dust for spurs. The scanty remnants of their pay would be carefully hoarded by the men and then dissipated in one night upon beer or the fiery, raw spirit, sometimes said to be doped with vitriol or other malignant mixtures, supplied by the canteen contractors. If the soldier had become inured to his coarse food so that he ceased to care as it was shovelled down, he discovered that he had begun to care for drink. Even if he was not allowed out of barracks there was nothing except lack of cash to save him from the fierce temptation of the canteen within the walls.[4]

The depressing little town really only came to life at night when the beer-shops were crowded to the doors with military drinkers. But they were topers with a difference in that they lacked the usual spontaneity of a drinker; in semi-restrained, low-voiced groups they raised and lowered their pots as if by numbers.[5] The late sun of the summer evenings did little to relieve the drabness of the narrow streets, even if it allowed the drinkers to lounge on benches outside the inns. They sat in an almost standard position – legs apart, forearms resting on the tops of the thighs, heads lowered with eyes reflectively contemplating the all-too-quickly vanishing ale in the pots held in front of the knees.

Because of the continual passage back and forth of officers, either in uniform or fashionable mufti and usually riding, the men were forced to rise to their feet and salute every few minutes. This they did with mechanical, marionette-like precision; in return for their efforts they received a careless flick of a glove in acknowledgement.

Sometimes when a man had finished his ale he would sit pondering as though seeking a decision; then he would suddenly rise to his feet and go looking for one of the bedragged tarts who nightly wore herself out for soldiers' coppers. Those who remained to drink themselves stupid or into an ugly mood would finish the evening with the inevitable brawl, followed by arrest for drunkenness and fighting.[6]

On the following morning they were marched in front of the Adjutant in the orderly room. Paraded stiffly by the Sergeant-Major, the cap was swept off the head in case the offender took it into his head to use the headgear as a weapon. The Adjutant would solemnly warn . . . 'that it was a bad beginning to a military career' and suggest the grimmest penalties for the next offence. The miscreant, in company with similar offenders, spent the next fourteen days of his leisure time on his hands and knees picking grass-blades from between the paving-stones around the square. A back-breaking punishment which had its own built-in soporific, causing the Corporal-in-Charge to accuse them of further idleness. This gained them extra punishment, a travesty of justice received without a murmur. Already in four weeks or so they had begun to acquire the wooden apathy that in the older soldiers eventually was brought to a pitch of fakir-like insensibility.

They were given musketry practice with antiquated firearms. The troop was formed up in a line forty paces from a whitewashed stone wall, the order given to blaze away at the discretion of the instructor until the allowed fifteen rounds per man had been fired off. The hits, if any, were counted, although the ancient muzzle-loading rifled firearms had been so long in use that their grooves had become obliterated and they were practically smooth-bores. They would have been extremely dangerous to carry loaded in a holster, as the balls worked loose and slipped down the muzzle.[7]

By now the recruits had mastered, after a fashion, the elementary foot-drill, sword exercises and musketry; they also were becoming painfully aware of the routine of barrack life. The time had come to begin their course of 'Military Equitation According to the Cavalry Regulations'. As the rule-book says:

'. . . consists in the skilful and ready application of the aids by which the rider guides and controls the horse in all its paces; and in a settled balance of the body which enables him to preserve a firm seat in every variety of movements.'

When these words were gabbled out to the recruits the whole business didn't sound too difficult, but there were to be many varied and painful movements executed before they acquired the desired firm seats. They were instructed in squads of eight or ten men, on horses with 'stripped' saddles and bridoons. The riding school was a long and gaunt, timber-walled building with a cobwebbed, bare brick arched ceiling; horizontal windows set high in the walls admitted only a dim light. The Rough-Rider Sergeant was a wiry, bowlegged man with a battered face and a vile temper; he was a man soured with his job and he delighted in giving the helpless recruits a rough time.

On their first day they were all finally mounted after several unsuccessful attempts; they were then punched, pulled and screwed into the correct riding position. Their bodies had to be balanced in the middle of the saddle; their heads erect; shoulders flung well back; small of the back slightly bent forward; thighs well stretched down from the hips, with the flats to the saddle; knees a little bent; legs hanging straight down near the side of the horse; heels lowered; toes raised from the instep . . . the instructions seemed never-ending and confused them mightily.

The recruits jogged endlessly round and round the school, with arms crossed and without stirrups. Like a militant ringmaster, the Rough-Rider Sergeant stood in the centre, brandishing a long whip. He would lunge first at this pupil and then at that one, flicking their bare hands and causing their mounts to rear and kick-up. He never stopped talking in a repetitive, mechanical manner:

'Sacks o' coal . . . roly-poly puddin's . . . I'll teach yer to ride . . . I'll make yer or break yer. . . . 'Ere! 'O gave you leave to dismount?'

This last remark was his parrot-cry on each and every occasion when a recruit fell off his horse – a very frequent event.

At intervals he would halt them and demonstrate what he wanted; on horseback he became even more formidable. He would come galloping in amongst them, upsetting them on all sides when they failed to accurately reproduce the movements he demonstrated on his own perfectly trained horse. The insecure seats were due to their inexperience but also because they were mounted on recalcitrant mounts with mouths hardened to insensibility by the cruel, long curved bits.

Before long the recruits were a sorry sight; faces and uniforms streaked with the tan into which they kept rolling; the insides of their knees worn raw and thigh muscles burning, they were also spotted with saddle-boils. Riding school became an even greater nightmare than the sword-exercise period; they knew no great terror than when the Rough-Rider Sergeant had the jumping hurdles erected and luridly described the horrors that lay before them.

But, as time went by, natural apitudes began to reveal themselves; their riding muscles became stronger and their balance improved. Some of the men caught the rhythm of the horse; the more slender pupils discovered a natural suppleness that served them well when it came to the higher and harder jumps. All this occurred in spite of the stiff long-legged poise on the stirrups and fork which was still the regulation cavalry seat, designed to give weight during charges. For some odd reason the lean, wiry townsmen showed the makings of better horsemen than the stockier, clumsy country-bred lads.

The Rough-Rider Sergeant did not seem to gain any pleasure from their improvement; rather he appeared to resent it and would show his displeasure by giving the recruits horses of known bad character. On these awkward mounts he would try to show up the recruit who had presumed to improve too quickly, terrifying the man with horses that reared up or fell over backwards.

At the beginning of December, in the presence of the Commanding Officer, they passed out of riding school. This part of the recruits' training was one that Lieutenant-Colonel McDowell always stirred himself to watch; he was a splendid horseman himself and a keen rider to hounds.[8] The Commanding Officer personally passed the men and would give grudging praise to any individual who performed a creditable 'in-and-out jump with sword cut at the Turk's Head'; those who did not come up to his requirements were rejected and sent back for a further course – with suitable stoppages of pay.

During the long months since they had joined up the recruits had seen much that was grim; the man with a background that made it possible dully to adapt himself to the degrading rigours of the life was able to soldier on, but the more sensitive suffered the tortures of the damned. Two of their comrades in the barrack-room, overstrained and underfed, succumbed to the conditions and sickened with typhus; taken to the dank hospital, they died in a few days. One of the two Irish recruits also became a casualty – but in a different way.

Long before they actually began riding instruction the recruits had been daily regaled by the older soldiers with stories grim and frightening – stories that they later found to be not exaggerated – of riding-school conditions. Tom Murphy dreaded this fresh ordeal so much that he steeled himself to commit the greatest of all military crimes – he deserted. By no means a good soldier, Murphy amazingly carried through this perilous enterprise with the skill of a master tactician so that not a soul could trace his movements except that he was present at Roll Call and 'Lights Out' one evening but had gone by 'Reveille' the next morning. Everyone was baffled by the way in which the big, clumsy, simple Irishman from County Tyrone had eluded the Corporal who slept in the barrack-room; passed the Main Guard without being challenged (although apparently in his uniform) and, without money or a pass, got clean away.

The Commanding Officer's fury was frightening: he reduced to the ranks the Corporal in charge of the barrack-room, put all the Main Guard under close arrest and had the remainder of the recruits paraded before him to be harshly lectured and warned. Aided by civil police and the railway detectives, mounted patrols scoured the countryside; identification notices were sent out to all police stations for miles around – but Private Trooper Tom Murphy remained free.

Now that they could ride they were introduced to the incredibly cumbrous system known as pivot-drill, a routine rarely mastered by very few men other than the actual drill instructors.[9] They found it indescribably difficult and infuriated instructors piled punishments upon their luckless heads. But they survived to excitedly pass round the news that Tom Murphy had been captured and was in the cells waiting the convening of a regimental court martial.

He had been taken by the Reading police whilst working as a farmhand near Pangbourne. He had been charged with desertion at Reading Police Court and an escort sent to bring him back; hair shaved off and manacled, he was roughly dragged through the camp. The older soldiers forecast that there was no doubt at all about the court's decision; they freely forecast that a very fierce example would be made of the Irishman as a lesson to the other recruits – leniency towards deserters was unknown.

4

Punishment for Man and Horse

A few days later, at dawn, the whole regiment paraded; they were dismounted and formed up in the three sides of a hollow square in the open space facing the riding school. It was bitterly cold and the dark winter morning cast an appropriate gloom over the proceedings. The gorgeously uniformed officers languidly strolled to the front of the regiment and they were called up to attention. The Commanding Officer appeared, attended by Major Rowland Smyth, the Second-in-Command, by Captain Dynon, the Regimental Adjutant, and by the Regimental Surgeon, Mr Sandham.

The silence of the raw morning was broken by marching feet; from the direction of the guardroom came a party led by the tall, superbly attired Regimental Sergeant-Major, followed by an escort of lancers in parade uniform bearing drawn swords. In their midst marched Private Trooper Tom Murphy, dressed in his uniform overalls and naked from the waist upwards; his flesh was purple and goose-pimpled with the cold. At the rear marched the lone figure of the Farrier-Sergeant bearing a cavalry whip in his hand.[1]

The escort and prisoner came smartly up to attention in the centre of the open space. Lieutenant-Colonel McDowell nodded to the Adjutant, who produced a document from which he loudly read the sentence of the court martial. He finished and marched to a position slightly behind the Commanding Officer; the escort moved up to the riding school where they lashed Murphy's wrists to the two iron rings fixed into the wall about six feet from the ground. They turned and marched back to their former position; Murphy was left spread-eagled, his bare back bluish against the rough red bricks. There was a deathly silence, broken only by the faint whistle of a distant train – then a harsh cry broke the stillness:

'One!'

There was a hiss like a blast of wind as the stroke was delivered 'as hard as could be, at the full length of the arm'; the thongs landed on Murphy's shoulders with a slapping thud that echoed back hollowly from the walls of the surrounding buildings. Murphy grunted.

'Two!'

The shirt-sleeved arm of the Farrier-Sergeant flashed down; again the spongy 'thud' filled the air. Murphy grunted again and dragged on his wrists; they had told him in the guardroom that it was a point of honour not to cry out under the lash and one of them had given him a 'piggy'. This was a small oblong of leather that looked as though a dog had chewed upon it:

'. . . this 'ere's a piggy, see? Yer grips it between yer teeth . . . 'ard . . . an' yer won't cry out.'

Another of the guards had agreed:

'An' yer won't bite yer tongue orf neither . . . ole Charlie Rose bit 'is tongue clean in 'arf and spit it out on the floor, didn't 'e?'

The weals that scored the flesh made an irregular scarlet track; mercilessly and monotonously the voice called out the number of strokes. Murphy was unable to choke back a shriek; the 'piggy' flew from his lips and he twisted on his bound wrists. His back began to resemble a fearsome map of red ridges; it was slowly turning the colour of raw liver. The Farrier-Sergeant ran the thongs through a rag after each blow to prevent them sticking together. The Irishman seemed to have lost consciousness under the punishment and his body swayed by the blows as it hung limply from the rings; he resembled one of the dummies that were used for practising sword-thrusts. The Surgeon suddenly threw up his hand; the Farrier-Sergeant paused with the whip uplifted over his shoulder, his face was free of any sign of lust or emotion – he was performing his duty to the best of his ability with the skill and rhythm of an expert butcher handling a carcass on the block. The Surgeon listened to Murphy's heart and fumbled at his bound wrists, seeking his pulse; then he stood back and nodded to the Farrier-Sergeant, who ran his tongue over his lips and again brought down the thongs.[2]

The sight, the noise of the lash landing on the bare flesh, the sickly sweet smell of blood that pervaded the crisp air, brought a tight feeling to the chests of the watching men. Some felt choked as though their breath was building up inside them and would cause them to burst; one man violently retched and was told to be quiet by a nearby Corporal; another went down with a crash, his lance-cap rolling away between the lines of stiff, spurred feet. Murphy's Irish mate, with whom he had joined, had lain awake half the night dreading this ordeal. Standing in the second line on the left-hand side of the square, he tried to shut out the sight by staring at the red, carbuncle-spotted neck of the man in front of him. But he couldn't shut out the sounds; he heard the voice of the man on his right, coming from a vast distance:

'Look at yer feet . . . only 'leven more.'

Ten . . . nine . . . eight . . . seven . . . the last strokes of the sentence of fifty lashes fell upon the dangling puppet. One of the escort flung a pail of icy water over the bloody mess that was Murphy's back; another cut him down, catching him under the armpits to take his dead-weight. The Irishman lay on the frost-rimmed ground with the Surgeon and the Sergeant of the Guard bending over him – they were tattooing his arm with the letter 'D' for deserter.[3]

The moral lesson having concluded, the Commanding Officer's voice rang out on the cold morning air:

'The 16th, the Queen's Lancers . . . form . . .'

His words were taken up by Troop Leaders in a chorus; the hollow square broke up and the regiment wheeled into a column that marched briskly past the limp body lying on the gravel at the foot of the flogging-rings. The officers sauntered off the area; most of them would be able to do justice to the eggs, chops and kidneys that awaited them in silver chafing-dishes on the long Mess sideboard.

It was customary for a parade to be ordered immediately after a flogging to take the men's minds off the event. As soon as they had arrived back in their barrack-rooms they were hurried through their sparse breakfast by their N.C.O.s and then given barely enough time to accoutre themselves and prepare their horses. To a march that lit up the grey, chill morning the regiment picked their way through the barrack gates. With stately step the piebald drum-horse paced at their head, drum-cloths displaying the cypher of Queen Charlotte with the Garter, and the motto:

'AUT CURSU, AUT COMINUS ARMIS' – 'Either in the charge or hand to hand'.

The Regimental Band looked splendid – despite the fact that the reversed facings and white tunics were forbidden they still managed to maintain a striking dress. Their horse furnishings were of lambskin edged with blue cloth – the colour of their full-dress facings; the saddle-cloths and drum-cloths bore the battle-honours of the regiment that had been raised in 1759 and converted into lancers in 1816.

Beaumont	Willems	Talavera	Fuentes d'Onor
Salamanca	Vittoria	Nive	Peninsular
Waterloo	Bhurtpore	Ghuznee	Afghanistan

The officers' shabraques were made with rounded ends; they displayed the Crown, Royal Cypher, crossed lances and regimental devices. The lance-caps had elaborate cap lines that finished on the chest with complicated founders and tassels; black cock's-tail feathered plumes drooped a full sixteen inches. All wore proudly the exclusive scarlet lancer jacket.[4] Set off by sleek flanks and combed manes, the gently jogging squadrons brought unexpected colour to the mean grey street of the little town.

For a full hour they performed complicated mounted evolutions on the Common until the mournful winter air was cloudily alive with the breath of 500 panting riders and horses. Each horse responded to its rider and each rider to his horse; they sat firm and upright in their saddles, responding immaculately to the brazen voices of the trumpets through which the Commanding Officer wielded his entire regiment as though it were a single troop. At last, tiring of such puppetry, the Colonel handed the regiment over to the Adjutant. It had begun to rain, so the regiment was ordered to break up into squadrons and carry on exercises under squadron commanders. The Adjutant hastily rode off to catch up with the Colonel, his master.

Through splashing puddles, mud and beating rain the horsemen careered until they were soaked to the skin and their lance pennants clung soggily to their shafts. The horses were breeched in slime up to the girths; the men's minds became full of the thought of the extra hours of cleaning and grooming that lay before them . Here and there horses fell while galloping across the greasy country; their riders, coated in mud and filth, were sent back to barracks to await punishment for being no longer fit to remain on parade.

The jumping field was a swampy morass dotted with hurdles and bars, with occasional sacks on poles for lance practice. The experienced sergeant-majors warned their officers that the ground was bad for horses at the jumps, to be told that battles weren't postponed on account of rain!

With heavy driving rain in their faces and slippery going under foot, the men found the jumps a hazardous procedure; the tired horses were going more slowly and taking the hurdles with difficulty. With their necks wearily extended, they scrambled over them rather than leaped. The men's uniforms and faces were spotted with mud clots that flew in all directions: the rain was increasing in intensity. The lance practice was almost out of the question, most of the men completely missed the target-sacks and those who hit often left their lances dangling forlornly from the stuffed bags as their sliding horses forced the long weapons from their grips.

Reluctantly attempting a jump, a horse slid forward suddenly, its forefeet slipped over the top bar. It turned a complete somersault to disappear with a sodden thump and a flounder of legs, then it reappeared, struggling to its feet and standing with drooping head and blowing nostrils. The rider lay motionless on the soggy ground. The Troop Sergeant galloped over and secured the riderless horse, inspected it for injury and then walked over to the immobile rider. After a short interval he remounted and galloped back to the Troop Officer; slightly breathless, he saluted:

'Afraid he's dead, sir. Horse rolled on 'im . . . think his neck's broke.'

'Right, S'ar'nt. Better send for the ambulance.'

The troop had heard it all and were looking sullenly at the Troop Officer. He wheeled his horse to face them and stood up in the stirrups:

'You think it isn't possible to make the round because of the rain and the slippery ground, but I'll show you that it was bad horsemanship not bad weather that killed your comrade.'

He snatched a lance so quickly from the nearest trooper that the man had difficulty in extricating his wrist from the leather thong. The officer couched the lance so that the point was down and made for the nearest jump. He completed the round of hurdles, making his point in all the sacks; as he landed after the final jump his little mare staggered so that he was half lifted from the saddle, but he did not fall. The officer arrived back in front of his troop, some of whom spontaneously cheered him.

'Silence! You see . . . I order you to do nothing that I am not prepared to do myself! Take them back to barracks, Sergeant.'

As they had expected, a lot of hard work was in store for them when they returned to barracks. In shirt-sleeves, with braces hanging down over the tops of their overalls, the men worked hard at their grooming; occasionally they would call the horses to come up or come over. The Troop Officers fastidiously sauntered along between the stalls, watching them work.[5]

Arduously and monotonously, life dragged on. It was difficult to assess which was the worst – the temperamental furies of their military superiors or the biased justice they had received from local magistrates before whom poverty and hunger had so often brought them. It was a far from happy period for the soldier; he was scorned and derided by the civilian population and demoralised by the severity and tedium of discipline coupled with the squalor of barrack life and the deadly monotony of countless hours spent on the drill-square.[6]

5

The Voyage to India

Cut off from the civilian world that lay outside their garrison town, the troops would colour their lives with the most lurid rumours of impending military operations. Some of the older soldiers had seen service in India and would regale their comrades with exciting stories of bloody battles in earlier wars.[1] The thought of active service was as breathtaking a vision as the convict might have of being released from prison. Anything was better than the drab monotony of their present existence; nevertheless, there was a real desire on the part of all ranks to take part in some glorious military episode which might well end in death or mutilation.[2]

They knew that trouble was brewing in India – it always was – and fervently hoped that they would be despatched to take part. Every day brought fresh rumours, and changes among the officers gave colour to the reports that they were shortly going overseas.[3] Even so, everyone was amazed and delighted when Lieutenant-Colonel McDowell addressed them on a regimental parade:

'Men of the 16th, the Queen's Lancers! I have some good news for you. The regiment is leaving here on Friday, We will be marching to the Isle of Sheppey from whence we will set sail for India. It is believed that the Sikhs, a highly disciplined race, intend to take up arms against Her Majesty's Indian domains. The 16th, the Queen's Lancers have been rightly considered to be suitable troops to handle such a situation. Good luck to all of you!'

For the next few days they lived amid a welter of orders, counter-orders, confusion and choas as the regiment prepared to vacate the barracks in which it had lived for many years. Full of seething excitement and tingling with martial spirit, they were led out of the barracks by the band. Watching them go were a crowd of wretched, wailing women with crying children hanging round their skirts. Whilst it might be possible for a proportion of wives and families to follow later, there was no certainty that many of the wives would ever see their husbands again.[4]

The cross-country march through the pleasant fields of Surrey and Kent was carried out under active-service conditions. Some of the men found that their excitement had been tardily replaced by the apprehension of the long sea voyage; few of them had even seen an ocean-going vessel before. They found that saying farewell to their horses was a sad business; many a head was turned back for a last look at the mounts they left standing in the field behind the quay.[5]

The ship on to which they filed under the bright, watery spring sun was a fully rigged sailing vessel – the *Maidstone* – of between 800 and 900 tons, quite a respectable-sized vessel for its day. It was owned by the Wygram Company of ship-owners, the rival of the still greater company of Green and Company. The *Maidstone* was commanded by Captain Peter Roe, an experienced and able sailor, who kept up the reputation of the old fast-disappearing class of vessels known as East Indiamen.

The anchor weighed, they were towed down the river until their sails could be of use; they were under sail before nightfall and made good weather throughout the following day. The men lined the rails, gazing on the green fields and white cliffs of 'dear old England'. They wondered whether they would ever see them again and when it would be. It was very much more pleasant on deck than between decks and as the ship neared the tropics the conditions below were to become even more repulsive. The crammed cabins, or dormitories, were so low that it was not possible, even if there had been enough room, for the smallest man to move about without bending his head and shoulders. The canvas hammocks were slung so close to each other that they touched, the whole lot swaying solidly as one when the ship moved. There was almost constant darkness and they were frequently awash with putrid bilge water that surged up and swirled through the corridors and cabins. Nearly all the men suffered badly from seasickness; it became an apparently permanent, mutual condition in which they all wallowed wretchedly. Cockroaches flew about, settling at times on their faces; they weakly pushed them off, but sometimes let them remain because they lacked the energy to do otherwise. From the moment they set sail until they dropped anchor four months later at Calcutta they lived to the eternal creaking rhythm of the ship's timbers, a grating noise that filled the air and became a part of them, like a ringing in the ears. They had been at sea for many days before they felt like eating, but found little to tempt their appetite. Salt pork, dry biscuit and lime-juice was to be their diet throughout the long voyage.

Crossing the Bay of Biscay the gales blew hard; when the men had to drag themselves from their hammocks they were usually so ill that they could hardly stand. The scene below was almost indescribable; the dim light made the pitching dormitory an animated mosaic of sick and straining men. The rolling from side to side of the ship made all the hammocks sway as one in a corresponding rhythm; above it all was the eternal creaking of the ship's timbers and the howl of the gale.

But the gale didn't last for ever and eventually the men became accustomed to the motion of the vessel; they began to take a renewed interest in life. There were few duties to occupy them there was no drill, but sometimes full-dress parades were ordered at the erratic whim of the Squadron or Regimental Commander. The trumpet would sound 'Fall-in!' and the men would hurriedly assemble in squadrons, each of whom had a certain allocated deck space. First they would be hectored and bullied by their N.C.O.s and then inspected by their officers; the Orders of the Day would be read out to them and then the officers would fall out. Eventually those other ranks who had not been detailed for some duty or fatigue were dismissed, usually to shamble aimlessly to the ship's rail where they would stand staring out over the limitless ocean as they talked to their mates. They sadly missed their pipes and tobacco.[6]

These dress parades inevitably brought in their wake punishments and reprimands; it was impossible in the crowded conditions that prevailed below decks for them to attire themselves in the correct and spotless fashion demanded by their superiors. The men vastly preferred the less formal parades when they would assemble in shirt-sleeves and with bare feet. Some of the men had been to sea before enlisting; banded with those more adventurous spirits among them they helped the sailors with the heavy canvas sails.

When approaching squalls led to the order 'All hands!' or even 'Watch shorten sail!' they would take their places with the reefers on the mizzen-top-sail-yard. They learned to lean far over the yard and pick up the reef points while the luffed sail flapped violently against their bare legs; sometimes their feet were almost knocked from the rope on which they stood. During the quieter hours this band would roam about the yards and upper rigging, the main-top in fair weather being a favourite place to rest. This climbing about gave them bodily exercise; it was an outlet for their pent-up energy which on board ship required a safety valve to prevent an explosion! Even so, explosions did occur – more than one savage fight took place with the fighters' comrades raucously urging them on. Such spectacles relieved the awful tedium of the dragging days.

They crossed the 'Line' and were becalmed for nearly a fortnight. This was a period which formed the most tedious and temper-trying time of the whole voyage. For hours, sometimes stretching into days, the vessel drifted about; sails barely flapped; there was not enough wind to keep a course. The breakfast rubbish thrown overboard from the ship's galley floated about the taffrail all day; it was often still there on the following morning. In this season there were generally other Eastern-bound ships in sight in these latitudes; the sailors did not like the vessels to get too close together. On the calm and painted sea when the ships approached near to each other they were apt to close in, being drawn together by the affinity which bodies of loose matter have one for the other when no counter-acting force is present to keep them apart. Signals were exchanged between ships but no communication by boat, although sometimes boats were had out to tow the becalmed ships. Those on the *Maidstone* had no option but to patiently await the occasional light winds which enabled them to keep steerage-way on the ship.

Below decks it had become insufferable as the heat became greater, and the men were permitted to sleep up on deck; this made life considerably more pleasant. But their existence was restored to its former state of semi-despair when the old wooden ship became infested with cholera; the slow monotony of their progress was punctuated by funerals at sea with depressing regularity. It seemed to be a very lethal type that had struck them; the Doctor possessed few medicines or preparations to meet such an attack and was unable to do very much to aid the stricken men. Within an hour of the first case being diagnosed a number of others had appeared; soon men were dying in contorted agony. The beds of the afflicted were taken to a prepared deck area and as soon as a man died his body was instantly weighted and cast overboard.[7]

Night fell, bringing with it drenching warm rain; the dreadful procession proceeded – from below decks, on to the deck and then into the sea with a mournful splash. By morning twenty-six bodies had been thus cast overboard. The next three days saw eighty more men down on the reeking deck, but it seemed that they were holding their own in better fashion than had the earlier victims. A few more died and went overboard, but the flame of the disease seemed to be burning itself out and at last there were no fresh victims. The sick men lay in the sun and were eventually taken below to recuperate; before the ship reached Calcutta they were shakily back on their feet.

They sighted the little islands of St Paul's and Amsterdam in the stormy seas of that far-off parallel of southern latitude. All ships bound for the Bay of Bengal followed the Western Trades as far as those islands; they then made a 'new departure' from them and turned towards the mouth of the sacred Ganges. It was nearly the end of September when they saw the low-lying mud-banks near the mouth of the River Hooghley.[8] More than once the ship anchored after taking a pilot on board at the 'Sand Heads'; finally they successfully passed the dangerous reach of the river known as the 'James and Mary'. The 16th, the Queen's Lancers had arrived in India.

6

Preparing for War

In an atmosphere of wild confusion made worse by the crowded conditions below decks the men gathered together their kit and belongings. They had been warned to parade for disembarkation at very short notice, although the *Maidstone* had been slowly wending her way up the river towards Calcutta for hours. There was a slight breeze coming off the water, which made it seem pleasantly warm without being too hot; even so, in full-dress uniform they found struggling up to the decks with their equipment to be fatiguing work that drenched them with sweat.

When they filed down the gang-plank at Calcutta it seemed that the heat closed in round them[1] and made unloading particularly trying; weeks without exercise coupled with the cholera epidemic had left them soft and weak. In the same uniforms that they had worn at Hounslow all through the previous English winter they became so fatigued that few of them felt any excitement or interest at once again setting foot on shore. They were not sufficiently alert to be aroused by the novelty of the Eastern country and the jabbering hordes of robed natives who surged around them. Some of the men collapsed, they were mostly those who had recently recovered from cholera; two men were struck down with heat apoplexy and one of them died within three hours.[2]

They had three hours of labouring on the dockside, followed by an hour of being fell-in; inspected; admonished; stood at ease; brought up to attention . . . 'as you were' . . . and all the other irksome military attentions that the presence of onlookers or a new site will arouse in officers and senior non-commissioned officers. With each man bearing his kit and weapons, they were wearily marched some miles to an ill-prepared camping site. This so offended the Commanding Officer that he had all ranks toiling ceaselessly for the remainder of the day until the place bore a vague resemblance to an ordered camp back in England. Tents were struck and re-pitched in meticulous lines, each troop and squadron being allocated their own particular area; stones were laboriously gathered and laid to form paths from officers' tents and regimental offices – later each stone would be painted and maintained a brilliant white. Finally, as dusk was fast falling, the cookhouse and latrines were organised in a far, out-of-sight corner of the camp.[3]

Now began a noisy carnival of orders, counter-orders, bullying, punishments and an occasional flogging as the regiment reorganised and refurbished. Apart from a few cases of heat-stroke, their health remained surprisingly good and they were fast becoming harder and inured to the new climate. But there was a tense, unhappy and restless atmosphere prevailing; all through the long months spent in the dreary voyage from England they had been buoyed up by the thought of military operations – every day spent on the banks of the Hooghley was to them time misspent. The young soldiers listened with open mouths to the tales of the older men who had been here before in some cases; they heard in their dreams the whistle of the bullet fired in earnest and the steady drumming of the horses' hooves as they came into line for the charge.

Small things assumed ill-proportioned importance; from officers downwards all raged for days when they were ordered to give up the long drooping plumes of cock's-tail feathers that hung from their lance-caps. Replaced by the simple black horsehair plume that was 'regulation lancer issue for India'. it was the only clothing concession made in consideration of the fact that they had left Europe and were now in an Eastern climate.

For the man in the ranks life was very boring; lower ranks were not allowed to roam around India seeing the sights, although the officers sallied forth daily and were soon busily engaged in a round of social activities.[4] In spite of sentries posted to keep them away, the camp was daily besieged by hordes of dirty hawkers and traders selling fruit, food and native-brewed liquor. The unwashed and often overripe fruit set off a wave of dysentery; the pies made of far-from-fresh meat brought food poisoning in their wake and the drink inflamed the men to acts of violence and incredible stupidity.[5]

The regiment was re-equipped with horses – an event which caused them the utmost pleasure and gave them a focal point on which their boredom and depression temporarily disappeared. They were mostly small mounts – Arabs and Persians standing only about fourteen hands or so; there were some bigger Cape chargers from South Africa and some 'Walers' from New South Wales, who were taken by the officers.[6]

A rumour spread around that they were to be supplied with carbines and the merits of these weapons as opposed to their present issue of pistols formed a great source of argument in off-duty periods. It turned out that there were none available, so they were never issued.[7] Life dragged monotonously on; it seemed that they had exchanged the bad conditions of the English cavalry barracks for similar conditions, but under a blazing sun into the bargain. All the old routines were accompanied by the same harsh unreasoning discipline; punishments were liberally dispensed and sullenly carried out. It almost seemed as though the unsuitable clothing and equipment which all ranks were forced to wear aroused a spiteful irritation in those giving the orders and resulted in anguish to those who took them.

Only one ray of hope seemed to exist; overriding all their irritations and boredom was the threat of war with the Sikhs.[8] Latrine rumours declared that the Governor-General, Sir Henry Hardinge,[9] and the Commander-in-Chief, Sir Hugh Gough, had insisted that the 16th Lancers were indispensable to the successful performance of any such conflict. But as the war (if it ever occurred) would by taking place over 800 miles away in the district Punjab, all had a nagging fear that it would begin and be finished before the regiment could get to the seat of operations! Then one monotonous day was enlivened and made different from those that preceded and followed it by the dramatic coming and going of gaily clad staff officers. As old soldiers know, latrine rumours frequently carry a basis of truth amid their guesswork, and this was to be no exception!

With the suddenness of a fuse being lit, the whole camp exploded into a strangely ordered chaos of movement, instructions, counter-instructions, orders, countermanded orders and rushing in all directions. Finally, a point was reached when from the seeming chaos emerged the firm fact that the regiment would assemble – with baggage – at 0700 hours on the 17th of October 1845 in readiness to march to Meerut.

7

Marching through India

The long march from Calcutta to Meerut was the most enjoyable period the men had experienced since joining the Army. In addition, it brought both man and horse back to the full physical fitness they had lost during the lengthy and debilitating voyage from England. Although march discipline was harsh and rigorously maintained,[1] there was much to soften its rigours as the long column wound its way like a red caterpillar across the Indian countryside. Best of all, except on the infrequent rest-days, there was no time for drill or sword exercises except for those men whom the zealous N.C.O.s considered below standard or whom they personally disliked; these unfortunates were put through lengthy and exhausting routines under the hot sun.

Only a small percentage of the officers and men had been on the march in India before this, consequently considerable difficulty was experienced in getting off. Many of the bullock-drivers deserted with their animals during the first few days; although the first day's march was only eight miles, it was sunset before the tail of the straggling column arrived safely in camp.[2] After three days on the road things settled down and no further trouble was experienced except with the baggage camels who were young and difficult to load in the dark. The day's march was usually about twelve miles; the regiment started out an hour before daylight and reached their next camping ground at about 10 a.m.; this procedure was not rigorously followed, however.

The country was flat like a billiard table and quite park-like in character. Although dusty, the road was very good and very straight. As the lancers passed through villages, the inhabitants turned out to gaze in awe at the long, gaily coloured column of horsemen, topped by fluttering red and white lance pennons, and and the multitude of camp-followers and baggage animals. Fine topes of mango and tamarind trees in the neighbourhood of the villages, each with a masonry-enclosed well, added much to the beauty of the surrounding countryside. They were told by the villagers and Indians with the column that pious men who had been successful in business often planted the groves and dug the attendant well for the benefit of travellers. To the weary men travelling along the dusty white Indian road during the hot part of the day such resting places were a heaven-sent blessing, even if only the officers and the non-commissioned officers were able to crowd into the shelter from the sun. Most of the men were able eventually to pour a bucket of water over their burning heads and the scorched napes of their necks.

At one stage of the march they came up with a much depleted English infantry regiment, also en route for Meerut. They had been deserted by their drivers, baggage animals and keepers when cholera had killed off some of the Indians and then spread through the regiment, affecting nearly a quarter of its strength. The enemy, more powerful than the soldiers of the Khalsa whom rumour said they were off to fight, had thinned the ranks of many regiments, both European and native, that year. It had stalked among the rough camps and the insanitary barracks along the Indus River insidiously and fatally, as it did every year, but this year was worse than usual.[3] In the form of a slow and wasting fever it had broken out among the English and the native regiments in most of the recognised stations – at Hyderabad, for instance, 2800 men were down altogether, At Karachi the 28th Regiment of Foot could only muster forty men fit for service out of the whole battalion, and at Sukkur, in Northern Sind, 1600 men were in hospital. There were only a few doctors to look after this army of sick men; although they had gained experience they were helpless and wearied in this constant battle against disease, sun-stroke and death that inevitably accompanied the Army in India.

With very vivid memories of their losses through the similar plague that had struck them on board ship, the cavalry were eager to get on ahead and leave this plague-spot behind them. But they were still too fresh out from England to be hard-hearted – after all, the infantry were their fellow-countrymen. Mr Sandham asked if one of his two assistant-surgeons, Mr Pilleau and Mr Currie, would volunteer to stay behind with a party of men from the 16th and help the stricken regiment, who had lost two of their three doctors with the disease. Ten men and Mr Currie remained behind and did their best; unfortunately their kindness rebounded because they brought with them traces of the disease when they rejoined the regiment four days later. So once again they felt the ravages of cholera; for more then ten days the first question that was asked each morning from man to man was – who had died during the night and who was dying. It was a terrible thing to be left behind with a dying man, waiting for him to breathe his last so that he could be buried and then the burial party hastened to rejoin the regiment, moving on ahead. They would sit in the shade, listening to the victim's heavy breathing; scanned closely by the vultures perched on nearby trees, waiting for their prey.[4]

Disease was not to be their only enemy; they had to cope with two intensely hot days, although the hot season was now well past. The soldiers unaccustomed to tropical heat, and lacking suitable uniform to defend them adequately from it, were wearing the red tunic and blue overalls they had in England; the small lance-cap gave no sort of protection to the neck. After forty-three men had crashed off their horses with sun-stroke, fourteen of them to be dead by evening, they were permitted to hang handkerchiefs over their necks. The sun's angry and aggressive heat seemed not only to scorch the head but to muddle and make chaos of the brain within it.

One day seemed to hotter than all the rest; tents had been struck and column of route formed under a fiercely hot wind that blew clouds of burning dust into the men's faces. It burned their skin and made their horses jib at facing into it. About a mile from their overnight camping place they came upon a squadron that had been doing outlying picquet; its general appearance was appalling. Two of its three officers lay helpless under trees with wet towels round their heads, and the men in an exhausted condition lay about in twos and threes under whatever shelter they could find. The Commanding Officer considered; he had a good sun-helmet with a long turban wound round it, yet the sun seemed to gimlet a hole through it into his brain. The very hair seemed to crackle from the burning heat, and the nails of the fingers became brittle and split. The Commanding Officer ordered a halt and the day was decreed one of rest.

Although the area through which they were moving was pleasant, they were eager to get further north where they were told the climate would be more temperate at this time of the year. Around them was a level, rich and well-cultivated province. The villages were built of sun-burnt brick of an ugly khaki colour, their walls being well scored by the heavy rains as they were exposed to every wet season; the doors and shutters were of the roughest carpentry. At sunset every evening the women and children assembled on the flat roofs to drink in the cooler air. Planted around the villages were some mango and tamarind trees and some of the detached houses of the richer people were enclosed by high kutcha-built walls. Many of the villages were loopholed and the large landowners lived in forts with deep ditches and hidden all round by some hundred yards of dense jungle. Scattered throughout the province were many fine tanks, surrounded by tall handsome trees and a Hindu temple or Mohammedan shrine; the surrounding groves were enlivened by numbers of monkeys or baboons chattering without ceasing during daylight. When the regiment camped or bivouacked in the shelter of these groves the men were highly amused and fascinated by the monkeys' cunning but solemnly performed antics.

The officers of the regiment were daily brought into contact with the people as they made inquiries about roads, the depth of rivers and the streams that had to be crossed, the whereabouts of bandits or bad men, and the common news of the locality. It became the firm impression of the inexperienced English officers that all the natives were liars by nature and habit. From suspicion as to the object of the questions, the natives endeavoured to mislead and, in fact, showed much ingenuity in the construction of their untruthful answers. On both sides there was confusion; the soldiers appeared to be under the impression that they would be more readily understood if they shouted, a habit which seemed to bewilder the natives. Not a man among the officers had the slightest knowledge of the language, nor had taken the trouble to learn even the simplest words during the long boring hours of the sea voyage.

With the advent of colder weather during the later stages of the journey, the last traces of sickness vanished. The men and the horses had become inured to the daily march, the outdoor life plus the enforced absence of drink making them harder and fitter than at any previous period of their military careers. The last day's march to Meerut lay through rich, grassy plains; the men's excitement increasing as they came in sight of the small town, with the military cantonments on its north extending for two miles. The place was in an uproar and the arrival of the cavalry regiment passed almost unnoticed. Rumours abounded on all sides.[5] One was told that the Sikhs had crossed the Sutlej and wiped out Littler's force at Ferozepor; it was said that the Sikhs had been destroyed by a large British force that had apparently sprung from the ground; and the Sikhs were reported to be fighting among themselves.[6]

Everyone seemed certain that there would be a war, that the Sikhs would be very quickly and decisively beaten and that a pleasant winter would be spent in Lahore by the troops. Spirits were high, the thought of active service served as a stimulant and a relief from the interminable days, months and years of barrack discipline.

8

Signs of Battle

At first the 16th Lancers were dismayed at the thought of doing a further long, fatiguing march so quickly on top of that from Calcutta. But as they caught the infectious war-spirit their grousing soon changed to eager anticipation. Their minds were probably changed most when they saw the wretched barrack accommodation that the troops were occupying. The lancers were living in tents on the outskirts of the cantonment, alongside their horse-lines, but dreaded being sent into barracks if they remained long in the area. They had already learned that much of the dreadful mortality in the British Army in India resulted from the barrack conditions.

For the first time they were mingling with veteran soldiers who had fought in numerous Indian wars.[1] The cavalrymen listened, entranced, to their tales of battle, blood and glory. They heard of the first siege of Bhurtpur, where the Rajah, having hurled back four British charges, built in his grey mud walls an immense new tower of the skulls of the British dead. Veterans of Napier's conquest of Sind told them the story of the red thread of honour – an event that had occurred in January of that year.[2]

It was heartening to the newly arrived lancers to hear their new comrades show such obvious admiration and affection for their commanders. Not a voice spoke anything but praise for 'Old Fagin' – gallant, pernickety yet purposeful Sir Charles Napier whose very appearance made the enemy shrink from him. He would always be at the threatened point in a huge helmet, large spectacles, long flowing hair, whiskers and beard, swearing at the top of his voice. Others praised the Commander-in-Chief, Sir Hugh Gough, whose orders had just arrived for them to proceed forward to Ambala and perhaps Ferozepor or the very frontier. 'Paddy' Gough had commanded many of those present in the Mahratta Wars; they approved of his courage and his thought for the men in the ranks; he was affectionately remembered for his fire-eating actions when he would place himself at the head of his troops and hurl them with fixed bayonets at the enemy without waiting for his guns to soften them up first.[3]

The days were filled with feverish activities and preparations for the long march and the fighting that would surely be at the end of it. Everything was done amid a fever of exhilaration that seemed to have gone like wine to the heads of all ranks; harshness and abuse had their edges dulled; the strictness of the officers and N.C.O.s was softened by a heavy, macabre banter. At last Sir John Grey, the commander of the force (a veteran of the Gwalior War), judged that everything was ready and on the 10th of December 1845 the huge array stood ready to move.

The force was composed as follows:

9th Lancers } each over 500 strong
16th Lancers }
3rd Bengal Light Cavalry
4th Irregular Cavalry
H.M.'s 10th Regiment of Foot (later the Lincolns)
Three regiments of native infantry
One company of sappers
Horse Artillery with two batteries (twelve 6 in. guns)

Numerically, the force numbered upwards of 10,000 men.

It was bright moonlight when at 4 a.m. the bugles sounded the shrill 'Reveille' to shatter the crisp, chill, silent night air. The seething, slumbering mass sluggishly heaved and stirred to their feet; the smoke of the night fires hung on the still air and everything stood out clear and defined. It was cold and the troops turning out from their blankets were in no mood to appreciate the picturesque effect made by the groups of sepoys, swarthy red-coated figures against a background of white canvas and a dark clear sky in the light of the fires they had revived with straw from their tents.

In all imaginable groups and positions the multitude of camels, horses and elephants groaned and cried as they stooped and kneeled for their burdens. The neighing of the hundreds of horses mingled with the shouts of the innumerable servants; their master's calls, the bleating of sheep and goats and, louder than all, the shrill screams of the Hindu women bewildered the senses.

The British troops were in high spirits as they formed up; the long uncertainty was at an end, they were not worried about the undoubted odds against them – British troops had always faced odds in India and won. They were in full dress – shakos, coatee, white cross-belts; sepoys wore scarlet cut-away jackets and white trousers with low black shako; lancers were in their high caps and cress accoutrements and the Bengal Light Cavalry were dressed like light dragoons. Perhaps the most picturesque were the Bengal Horse Artillery, a *corps d'êlite*, the men being the pick of those recruited by the Company, of magnificent physique and with a distinctive uniform. The jacket much the same as that worn by the Royal Horse Artillery in later years, but instead of the busby they had a brass helmet covered in front with leopard-skin, surmounted by a long red plume which drooped over their backs like that of a French cuirassier; with white buckskin breeches and white gloves they were colourful if not particularly practical.

The camp-fires, around which the shivering camp-followers congregated, began to expire. The camels' roar continued to compete with the babel of tongues, but all other sounds were being drowned by the heavy tramp of feet as the troops moved off in column of route. There were blank-faced British infantry side by side with tall, swarthy men from the Ganges and Jumna; the Hindu, the Moslem and white man, all marching off for the same purpose. The quiet-looking, English-dressed native troops and the British cavalry contrasted strangely with the Irregulars in all the fanciful un-uniformity of their costume.

Grey-headed subahdar and light-hearted ensign, all pointed to the unmistakable fact that it was an Indian Army on the march. The whole assembly totalled approximately 10,000 fighting men, 38,000 followers and 30,000 camels, elephants and horses.[4] The long baggage trains of an army were much the same all the world over except in India, where elephants and camels took a major part. It must have been a similar sight to the Greek soldier as he followed Alexander the Great when he pressed forward towards the Jhelum. The same glitter from bright weapons, the same tramp of men, neighing of horses, beating of drums and braying of trumpets, the similarly caparisoned elephants, the same grunting, overladen camels.

As the day wore on the heat became trying: the dust was stifling and the pace only from one and a half to one and three-quarter miles an hour. The road had been worsened by recent rains and all combined in cursing the engineer who had constructed it.

The engineers went ahead in order to bridge rivers and make

up the roads where necessary so that the columns could proceed without delay. Then came the cavalry, followed by the infantry. The length of the column of march extended over several miles; there were thousands of camels and pack animals, dhoolies for the sick and wounded, spare horses and crowds of attendant syces on ponies.[5] The men's packs, bedding and ammunition had to be carried, together with food and cooking equipment; the commissariat required a vast number of native carts called hackeries, each drawn by two bullocks.

The passage of the River Jumna provided a wonderful study of perspective; column after column forded the river, their bright scarlet shining in the sun which flashed off the bright steel of bayonets, lance points and swords, to flicker through the clouds of dust. Long trains of bullock hackeries, the elephants, camels, doolies, staff officers, commissaries, the artillery with straining horses and swarms of camp-followers with a mighty impedimentum of baggage all pouring down towards the river. Following in parallel lines the folds of the serpent-like column of the army ascended the opposite bank to disappear in the jungle on the horizon.

Day after day the march progressed uneventfully, with the infantry trudging mile after mile through dense clouds of dust raised by the shuffling feet of the many thousand humans and animals. In spite of the white dust that lay thickly upon everyone, the cortège was a colourful and impressive sight. Against the drab earth-coloured background, the colourful oriental garb of the Irregular Cavalry vied with the bronzed infantry's white cross-belted scarlet. The sun's rays glanced off steel weapons, occasionally to strike the eyes of the plodding cavalrymen, lance-pennons drooping above their heads. Along the dusty road slowly wound the hundreds of loaded camels, the elephants, horses, bullock-carts with their guards and drivers. Had the Sikhs been close enough to see it, they might well have thought that they were being invaded by a handful of men backed by an army of animals!

The column reached Ambala on Christmas Day; it was comparatively deserted and they were told by the few troops remaining how Sir Hugh Gough had marched out on the 12th of December. This was the day on which the Sikhs had crossed the River Sutlej and two days after Sir John Grey's force had left Meerut, it was the first they had heard of the Sikh aggression. The force was given a mere day's rest, during which they reorganised their transport and arranged for some of the invalids and march casualties to remain behind. On the 27th of December the column set off on their 160-mile march to Ferozepor, near the frontier, and the likely area in which they would do battle with the Sikhs.

The country over which they had to march was dead flat, overgrown with camel-thorn and low jungle trees, but without any undergrowth. The roads were mere tracks, sandy and dusty, better suited for camels than for men who had to laboriously pick each foot up out of the dust as though marching through deep snow. The force were slowly moving through the heavy country in an irregular square. Without any knowledge of the situation forward, or whether the Sikhs were advancing towards them, such a defensive formation was probably safest, although it made marching even more difficult. The men and carts had to move in the ruts made by the closely grouped formation ahead of them; it was most unpleasant because of the dust and difficult underfoot conditions.

They slowly trudged over the country where the sand and jungle alternated with ploughed land, where the thickest dust obscured the air until day was turned into night. During the day the hot sun beat down upon the heavily burdened men, but the nights were bitterly cold. The infantry marched in line on one of the square's irregular sides, with the cavalry opposite, and parallel to them; both attempted to preserve their camping distance from each other and to keep the heads of the columns abreast of each other. The advance guard, consisting of all the picquets coming on duty, protected the front face; at the back the picquets coming off duty formed the rearguard. Inside the square next to the infantry the artillery moved on the rough road; the remainder of the space was occupied by baggage, cattle and camp-followers. They camped each night as they marched, for the most part, the infantry and cavalry facing outward in their two lines so that they afforded protection to everything within the enclosure.

There were very few villages and little or no water except from the wells dug by the villagers. Food was getting scarce; owing to the need for haste there was little time or means to cook rations or meat, a circumstance which particularly weighed upon the native troops – the Hindu being a ceremonious feeder.[6] The force marched 18 miles to beyond Rajpura on the first day after leaving Ambala; 16 to Sirhind on the next day; then 20 to Isur; 30 miles in a deadly tiring march to Lattala; 15 miles to Basseen on the next day and then a further 15 to Wadni – over 100 miles in six days. At Wadnī they found a small force that had been left to garrison the mud fort, captured from the Sikhs by Gough's force a fortnight before. They did a short march on the following day to Charrack, thus giving the weary men and beasts some rest. The whole march up from Ambala had been exceptionally rapid and through the most trying country. Bad weather hit them on the following day and the country soon became a quagmire as the rain fell in torrents. The road, no better than a bullock-track, could scarcely be traced; all was bog and mud and swamp. The gun wheels sank beneath their axles and the artillerymen pushed and pulled in the mire; the infantry slipped and slid and fell and fell again, wet to the skin, covered in dirt and sandy mud that rubbed them raw as they marched. The horses of the cavalry stumbled and swerved, blinding their riders with the mud they struck up; the baggage camels sprawled in the slime. Panting and cursing, they dragged themselves on in alternate periods of fierce sunshine and blinding rain; wallowing in filth, the men ploughed their way through nine miles of country before a halt was called.

They rested on the following day; this was a good thing because all agreed that the next day's march was one of the most harassing of the whole journey. They were at one time over heavy-ploughed land, then through low thorny jungle which broke up all order, then again over heavy sand – the most fatiguing ground of all for any army on the march. The rising dust was blinding, and clogged the throats and nostrils. Finally, the column arrived at a small typical Punjab village, with mud walls and houses; there was a well and a ramp for well-buffaloes, and a mill where a blindfolded camel would walk round and round. In front of the village was a tank to which men and horses and camels dashed impetuously under the pressure of an insatiable thirst. Discipline was suspended as men and horses rushed pell-mell to the tank and fought to push their faces over its edges. The stragglers were stretching for miles in the rear and came dragging wearily in as the troops began to prepare a meal. The area on which the force halted to rest and eat had obviously been used recently for the same purpose. Abandoned items of equipment lay about on all sides, much of it appeared to have been left behind as if the troops had evacuated in a great hurry.

After they had eaten and rested, some of the men wandered off to explore the small mud fort and deserted village; they came tumbling out of the fort shouting excitedly. Everyone wearily dragged themselves to their feet and drifted across to stand, open-mouthed, laboriously spelling out the names roughly inscribed on the crude wooden crosses erected over sandy humped graves. At a rough count there seemed to be over 200 of them, indicating that a severe engagement had taken place in the vicinity.[7] There was Private Mike O'Reilly of the 50th Foot; Private Tom Maggs of the 9th Foot; Corporal W. Judd of the 31st Foot and Sergeant Peter Hunt of the 80th Foot – all killed in action on the 18th of December 1845, with many more of their comrades from the four of Her Majesty's Foot Regiments that had left Ambala with the Commander-in-Chief on the 12th of December. On one side of the improvised burial ground was a separate group of graves containing cavalrymen of the 3rd Light Dragoons, who had obviously suffered very heavily. Inside the fort were littered heaps of torn and stained uniforms, pieces of marked equipment and bloodstained bandages; the place had been turned into a hospital by the look of things.

The bugles blared out the assembly call; buzzing with talk, the men hurried back to clean their equipment and form up for the rest of the day's march. Doubly alert by the knowledge that the Sikhs had been in the neighbourhood, they trudged in the defensive oblong through the thick sand towards a belt of dense low jungle, skirted by the track on which they were moving. Approaching the trees and undergrowth it was possible to distinguish a maze of copses and sandhills blending with the jungle; and there were increasing traces of the battle that had been fought on the 18th of last month. The ground was littered with shattered muskets, torn clothing, ripped-open knapsacks, scraps of paper and pages of letters. On all sides lay bones cleaned by the vultures and bleached white by the sun. The bulk of the battle had been fought on the edges of the low jungle, although many grisly relics probably lay within the dense confines of the low, stunted trees and interwoven undergrowth. Many bodies had been left unburied. Tattered remnants of clothing and the turban cloths indicated they were Sikh soldiers, although bones are white whether they have come from European or Asiatic. A louder buzz of excitement arose from the slowly marching force when they caught sight of a number of half-wrecked, dismantled cannon, with muzzles queerly angled and pointing crazily out from the trees. The artillerymen gave their professional opinions:

'Those ain't no British guns – they're twelve-pounders o' the Sikes.'

It did not take much military experience to work out that this had almost certainly been a British victory. There was a lack of wrecked British guns or large equipment, showing that they had remained masters of the field and were able to remove their damaged material after the battle had ended. The numbers of Sikh guns lying wrecked in the jungle showed it to have been defended by them and attacked the British and native infantry. Mounds of horses' bones and carcasses indicated a considerable cavalry mêlée on the flanks. The marching troops scanned the terrain with narrowed eyes, estimated distances and judged troop movements with professional eyes.

Only the officers with maps knew that this was Mudki, a battlefield where, on the shortest day of the year 1845, Sir Hugh Gough had beaten the Sikhs. It was a confused affair amid dust, smoke and fading daylight; although the British won a decisive victory their losses were heavy.

The force encamped a couple of miles further on in an area still strewn with enough discarded equipment and remains to indicate that a pursuit had taken place over the ground, towards Ferozepor. Next morning, the 6th of January 1846, they were aroused before first light. By dawn the camp was struck, packed on camels and an hour later the whole force was formed up in line of columns ready to march. Sixty rounds of ball ammunition were served out to each man and two days' cooked rations ordered to be carried in the haversack; the leather-covered water-bottle was slung over the shoulder. The infantry were clothed in their ordinary scarlet uniform with blue trousers, their forage caps were covered with white cloth and had a curtain hanging down behind for protection of the head and neck. Greatcoats were left with the men's packs to be transported on baggage animals, so that the troops could march light and unencumbered in case of sudden action. In line of columns they slowly advanced for about four miles. The force were ready to deploy into line in case the Sikhs should be encountered but when advance cavalry patrols reported they could see no signs of the enemy they changed to column of route, left and front.

They made very slow progress on a road that was a mere track cut through the jungle. In the opinions of many with vivid recollections of what they had seen on the previous day the column was dangerously stretched out. It took six hours to traverse a few miles and all were glad when at noon they emerged on to a broad expanse of level plain, dotted here and there with low jungle. In the distance a mud Punjab village could be seen; it had a few high houses standing up in its centre; the word crept along the column that this was Ferozeshah. They halted for a scratch meal from their haversacks; short of rations they were now eating 'elephant's lug' – a coarse cake made of wholemeal, molasses and chopped straw, the usual elephant ration! Here were signs of another battle, the whole area was littered with scattered and broken equipment, shattered muskets, torn and bloody clothing. There were wrecked guns and limbers surrounded by the bones of dead horses picked clean by the vultures, although piles of charred fragments showed that attempts had been made to burn the carcasses of the horses.

It was a bigger battle-field than that of Mudki. The village was a shot-torn shambles, not a house possessed a whole roof and the walls were riddled with the huge gaping holes that roundshot tears. There were large numbers of wrecked and spiked guns lying on all sides, big Sikh guns at that – if the lads had had to storm those entrenchements in the face of that artillery then they'd most likely taken heavy punishment. The artillerymen solemnly nodded their heads, pointing out that these guns were twelve-and eighteen-pounders, with even an occasional twenty-four- or thirty-pounder in evidence; we'd nothing much heavier than the nine-pounders that had been re-bored from the six-pounder with bad effects on range and accuracy.

They reached the camp area and settled down, tended the horses and put out picquets. Then they walked out on to the field of battle to view the place. The stench was horrible; large numbers of dead were buried in shallow scraped graves only a few yards from the camp and piles of dead in various stages of decomposition could be seen lying around the heaps.[8] In one place they came upon parties of the 3rd Light Dragoons and Sikhs lying together; they must have fought hand-to-hand after their horses had fallen. On the following morning, when the main body moved off, a party of the 16th Lancers were left behind to bury all the Europeans they could find. This was a most unpleasant task and the retching men worked hurriedly under the flaming sun to get it done as quickly as possible. They came across some ghastly tableaux such as the three abandoned Sikh guns, gunners lying where they had fallen, their legs thrown across their horses. They were in battery, and had obviously been doing great execution to the British facing them when some British infantry had got on their flank just as they were trying to move off and had dropped the whole lot of them with one volley.

Sir John Grey's force marched on towards the main army;

they now knew that they were going to be very welcome reinforcements to a battered, if victorious, army – an army that would have many a tale of glory to tell them around the camp-fires. The battle-fields behind them, their depression lifted in the bright sunshine, they suddenly felt very brave and full of fire – they'd show them Sixes what was what! A distant cloud of dust aroused interest and a patrol was sent forward to investigate, whilst the column, without actually halting their march, prepared for action. The dust-cloud grew larger, it was obviously cavalry moving fast towards them; the lancers comfortingly gripped the smooth shafts of their lances, loosened their swords in their scabbards and unbuttoned the flaps of their pistol holsters. They recalled the 3rd Light Dragoons whose bodies they had seen earlier, and imagined themselves in a dashing charge that would take them right through the lighter Indian cavalry! To their disappointment it was a body of friendly horsemen – the advance guard returning with a group of strange staff officers and their cavalry escort. Then the disappointment was replaced by excitement as they realised that these men were from Gough's army, they were the veterans of the two battle-fields they had seen – and that meant that they had nearly arrived up with the main army!

The sun became less hot and heads were held higher, the roads suddenly were less dusty and hearts were lighter. The whole tedious aspect of the march altered; only five more miles! The word spread down the column like wildfire – five more miles and they would be with the lads! The distance went by in the lightest-hearted and easiest manner of the whole march, until they came in sight of the lines of white tents coloured in pastel shades by the glory of the rapidly setting sun – it was the British camp at Arufka.

Sir John Grey's force could see the camp begin to come to life like a disturbed ant-heap. The area pulsated and throbbed with dark shapes moving in their direction. The area of sandy, shrub-dotted and arid land between them and the camp soon became black with troops. These European and native soldiers in various states of off-duty undress, who cheered them heartily, broke into their ranks to shake their hands and carry their weighty 'Brown Bess' muskets over the last few yards of their 280-mile march. The camp had the appearance of a lively and populous city amidst the wilds of solitude on the dreary plain. It was methodically laid out in regular, regimental 'streets', contrasting strangely with the haphazard camps of the thousands of followers, baggage-men, drivers and the like, that stretched beyond it. A regimental band gaily played them in; its martial strains made them automatically straighten up, look to their dressing and hold their heads higher. The column reached the large open space in the middle of the camp and were halted, formed into a square with one side open, and called up to attention. To a sharp 'Present arms', Sir John Grey rode forward, dismounted and saluted the Commander-in-Chief, who had advanced in front of a group of his staff officers.

General Sir Hugh Gough, Commander-in-Chief of the British Army in India, was a stocky, well-built man in his late sixties. Bushy white hair swept back from his high, bald forehead, and a full-white moustache, with eyebrows to match, gave him a benevolent expression. He had put on his white 'fighting coat' for the occasion, or perhaps to shield himself from the chill of the Punjab winter evening.[9] In a rich Irish brogue he addressed them:

'Well, my lads, you're very welcome, very welcome indeed. We've had a couple of very good shindigs with the Sikhs while we waited for ye to come up – and we won 'em both, ye'll be glad to know. The last one was a close-run thing, mark ye, not that I ever had any doubts about it! I knew that British troops with cold steel would rout any enemy the Good Lord provided for us. We left a lot of good lads on those bloody fields an' I know you'll all do your best to fill up the ranks. God bless ye all!'

The bands crashed into the National Anthem; every man stiffened and became an immobile statue, his fatigue forgotten. The last heart-touching strains died away; the newly arrived force spontaneously burst into uncontrollable cheering that split the rapidly darkening Indian sky. Every man cheered his heart out; every man felt that he was a part of something much bigger than himself, something that made him feel warm inside – a nice comforting warmth.

9

Paddy Gough's Army

On the 7th of January, the day following their arrival in camp, Sir John Grey's force were allowed to rest; much of the day was spent listening in respectful silence to tales of the two bloody battles that had been fought by the hardened veterans amongst whom they now rested. Mouths opened wide in awe when told of the heavy Sikh guns, fired and defended to the last by well-drilled gunners with rum flasks strapped to their wrists; gunners who died fighting fiercely to prevent their beloved guns being captured. The new arrivals were warned about '. . . them bloody native sepoys we're lumbered with . . .' and told how '. . . they were frightened to death of the Sixes . . . so's they got in a panic when the 50th Foot went past 'em an' they fired into our own lads!'

Gough's men sympathised heartily over the awful route to Mudki from Ambala; recalling how they had sunk down exhausted in Mudki to prepare a meal which they had to leave uneaten as they rushed out to meet the surprise approach of the Sikh army. The story was told of the Horse Artillery going right into the dense jungle to get their lighter guns into range of the Sikh heavy cannon. They heard of the dashing charge of the 3rd Light Dragoons – everyone now called them the 'Mudkiwallahs'; and they thrilled at the thought of the fierce and desperate fighting in the dense jungle when failing light and the choking dust made friend fire upon friend. Men who had yet to come under fire chilled at the grisly tales of what the Sikhs did to the wounded; each man resolved to save the last bullet for himself. But, however hard the fight at Mudki might have been, all agreed it was a picnic compared with what took place at Forozeshah three days later.

Commencing with a difficult march, everything seemed to go wrong at Ferozashah. The men were fourteen hours under arms, with little food or water, even before the battle began; the Governor-General would not permit Sir Hugh Gough to attack before the arrival of Littler's force from Ferozepor. The Sikhs were well entrenched in a fortified position with over 100 heavy guns and 35,000 men; the British had 17,000 men and fewer guns, which were also smaller in weight.

Littler's infantry suffered heavily in the battle's early stages – the 62nd Regiment losing 260 men. After this repulse Sir Hugh Gough personally led the attack of the right wing, Sir Henry Hardinge similarly leading the centre attack. A desperate struggle ensued as the British and native infantry fought their way through the felled trees in the ditch before the Sikh's walled position. Sir Harry Smith pushed forward with his division and by nightfall was in the Sikh camp about a mile in advance of the rest of the British army. He fought his way back during the night and re-joined Sir Hugh Gough early next morning in time to fight on the second day of the battle.

The long cold night hours were unforgettable. Sikhs wandered the battle-field murdering the wounded; guns roared from the blackness, scattering death among the exhausted, sleeping soldiers. On one occasion the Governor-General personally led the 80th Foot to silence a gun that was causing them casualties. When they returned he told them that they were 'Plucky dogs! We can't fail to win with men like you . . .!' Throughout the endless night both Hardinge and Gough constantly toured the round bivouacs, cheering and encouraging their men.

When the mist of early daylight lifted it was seen that the Sikhs had reoccupied their entrenchments. Sir Hugh Gough and Sir Henry Hardinge placed themselves at the head of their depleted force and with a loud cheer they went forward over the wall and through the Sikhs, who turned and fled. The victorious but exhausted British army rested on their muskets, only to see a fresh Sikh force, as large as the one they had just defeated, appear on the horizon. Almost without ammunition, shot or shell, the British prepared to sell their lives dearly. Unable to reply, the infantry stood in formation under heavy fire from the Sikh guns; Sir Hugh conspicuous in his white 'fighting-coat' rode forward alone to draw the fire off his beloved soldiers.

By an incredible error the horse artillery and the cavalry rode off the battle-field, having been given orders to retire by a staff officer half-crazed by shell-shock. The nervous Sikh commander mistook this for a threat to his flank and after firing a few more shots the whole force took themselves off and left the battle-field to the British. In the words of General Havelock: 'We were saved by a miracle'; Sir Henry Hardinge expressed the view that 'Another such victory will cost us the Empire!'

The arrival of Sir John Grey's Meerut force of 10,000 men had greatly strengthened the army, which was now about 25,000 strong, and on the 12th January Gough shifted eastward so as better to command the passages of the Sutlej. He sent Brigadier Godby to Ludhiana with the 30th Regiment of Native Infantry, a regiment of native cavalry and the Sirmoor and Nusseree battalions of Gurkhas.[1] This force was ordered to hold the fort; the bungalows of the civil and military residents at Ludhiana having just been burnt by a raiding party of Sikhs. Sir Harry Smith's Infantry Division and Cureton's Cavalry Brigade were posted on the right at Mkhu; the main body of the army was in the centre over against the Sikh position at Sobraon; the left was at Attari, preserving communications with Ferozepor.

The newly arrived regiment of lancers had been posted to the Cavalry Brigade under Brigadier C. R. Cureton, which was in support of Sir Harry Smith's division.[2]

The inexperienced lancers learned more about outpost duties in a few days than they had ever previously dreamed of. Brigadier Cureton knew his job and expected all those under him to be in the same happy position. Life was infinitely more pleasant than had ever seemed possible during those far-off days in English barracks and on the troopship. They were on active service in a foreign country, and glory lay just round the corner for all to grasp. A man could show his true worth and courage with a minimum of the humiliating and soul-destroying restriction and discipline of home service.

It was no secret that Sir Hugh Gough and the Governor-General were anxiously awaiting the arrival of the heavy siege train from Delhi. It was a battering train of guns of a calibre and weight far in excess of anything that they possessed at Mudki and Ferozeshah. With these guns Sir Hugh Gough was in a position to soften up the Sikh defences before launching his sorely tried troops at them with the bayonet. He would have parity in artillery, and Pyrrhic victories such as he had recently obtained would be replaced with a definite success that would end the war. In spite of his faith in the efficacy of cold steel Sir Hugh Gough had been badly shaken by the heavy losses of his British troops. Hitherto he had found little use for such subtleties as artillery barrages, but now he felt very inclined to take the advice of his divisional commanders and soften up the enemy with gunfire before throwing in the infantry with the bayonet.[3] This meant that the most essential item in his future plans was the long column that was taking up ten miles of road on its way from Delhi. Not only did it include guns and ammunition but also treasure with which to assure the loyalties of some doubtful Indian allies on the fringes of the war.

The Commander-in-Chief and the Governor-General were very anxious about this convoy. It contained the only guns in the country of the type they needed; if they fell into enemy hands it could possibly cost the British the campaign. They were in constant touch with the convoy by courier and its slow and frustrating movement along the dusty roads was followed with apprehension and nervousness.

Then came alarming news – a force under Runjoor Singh, consisting of about 8000 men and some seventy guns, had crossed the River Sutlej at Phillaur, about six miles north of Ludhiana. They had established a bridgehead by constructing entrenchments and occupying an old fortress in the vicinity. This latest, well-conceived Sikh move was most worrying; an intelligent tactical handling of their force could throw the precious convoy into danger. It seemed that it might have a good chance of succeeding unless nipped in the bud at the very beginning; the Sikh army was already in a position seriously to threaten the Delhi convoy. In addition to this objective it appeared that the Sikhs intended to garrison the forts of Dharmkot and Fatehgahr – the former being midway between Ludhiana and Ferozeshah and the latter about twelve miles to the east of Gough's present position. At the same time the Sikhs were covering that part of their army which was collecting much needed supplies from the Sikh State of Jaghir.

Sir Hugh Gough, Commander-in-Chief, and Sir Henry Hardinge, Governor-General, put their heads together and decided that Sir Harry Smith possessed the right sort of aggressive spirit and was capable of sufficiently inspiring a relatively small force so that they would hold the Sikhs at bay whilst the convoy got through.

10

The Frustration of Sir Harry Smith

So on the 16th of January 1846 Sir Hugh Gough sent for Sir Harry Smith; he told him that the Governor-General urgently required that the two fortresses taken over by the Sikhs be reduced. The Commander-in-Chief suggested:

'I think a brigade of infantry will be sufficient to send, together with the 3rd Light Cavalry and some Irregular Horse – whom will you send in command?'

Characteristically, Sir Harry replied that he would go himself, and turned to go. Sir Hugh called after him that there was no real hurry; Sir Harry answered briskly:

'Soon after this time tomorrow I shall be writing my report that I have reduced them both.'

Gough laughed:

'Why, the distance to Dharmkot is twenty-six miles from your right!'

Harry Smith was well aware of this fact:

'I know that, sir. Still, what I say shall be – provided that the officer of the engineers supply me in good time with the powder I shall want to blow in the gates in case of necessity.'

Sir Harry Smith believed in following the maxim of his former master, the Duke of Wellington – waste not a minute! Collecting everything that he wanted from what was left in the camp, he marched out two hours before daylight. He found Fatehgahr abandoned, so pushed on to Dharmkot, which he found occupied by the enemy who were without artillery. As his infantry had not yet come up, Sir Harry invested the fort with the 3rd Light Cavalry and the Irregular Cavalry. He parleyed with the garrison commander and gave him twenty minutes to surrender, with the promise:

'You may march out with your arms, ground them on the glacis, and I will endeavour to secure all hands six weeks' pay.

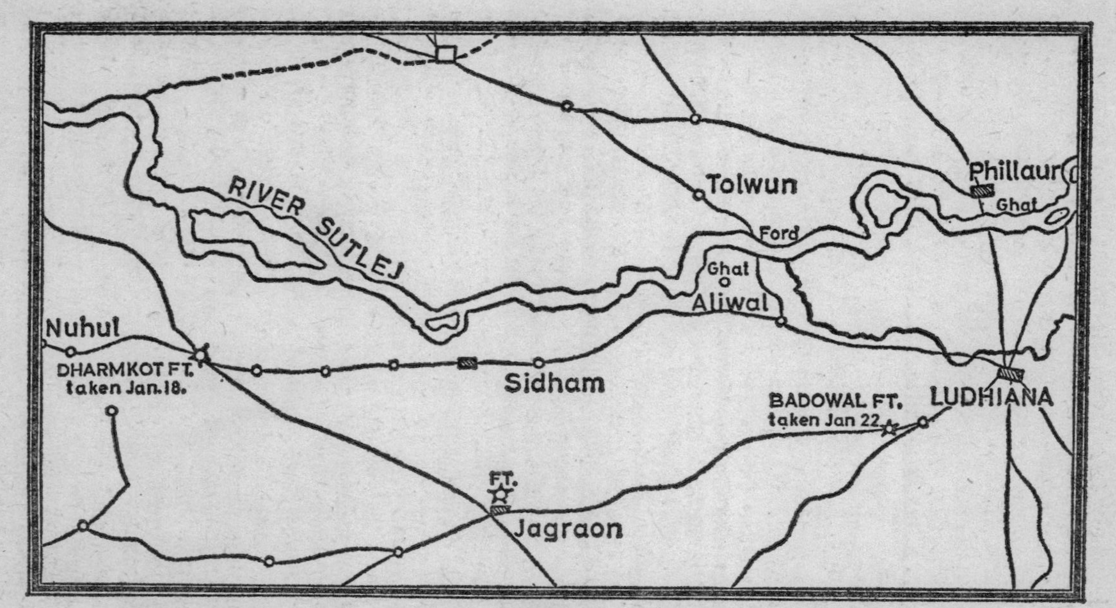

MAP TO ILLUSTRATE SIR HARRY SMITH'S MOVEMENTS IN JAN. 1846

Go back to the fort. I give you twenty minutes to consider, after which I shall make no terms but open my cannon upon you.'

A few shots eventually had to be fired from the nine-pounders and the howitzer, then the Sikh flag came down and a white flag fluttered sullenly up. The enemy marched out, and were taken off as prisoners of war by the British infantry who had marched up. The fortress was occupied and put into a state of defence. After their long march of the previous day the force rested on the 18th of January. On the same day a message was received telling Sir Harry that he was to receive on the following day reinforcements. Consisting of the 16th Lancers, the remainder of the Irregular Horse and two troops of Horse Artillery (twelve guns), this small force was under the command of Brigadier C. R. Cureton.

The 16th Lancers moved in column out of the camp under the eyes of their envious comrades who called out good wishes to them. Up the slight slope from the eastern side of the camp and over the crest of the small hill they rode, on to the flat plain that lay ahead of them. The horizon was beginning to tan and smoulder with the ashy colours of fresh sunlight. At first they were slumped in their saddles, but life gradually come to them with the sun's warmth and their muscles were loosened by the steady jogging. They rode to the accompaniment of the usual sounds of moving horsemen – the squeak of leather, the jangling of metal equipment, the soft, almost soundless plodding of the horses' feet in the deep dust. It was a lullaby broken only by the occasional murmur from one sleepy man to another and a horse's sudden snort.

The column progressed with an elastic stretching, sinuously following the contours of the land; they had flank guards to right and left and advance points far ahead – Charles Cureton knew his job. Everyone settled down to what they realised was going to be a long and hard ride; they were to be hard-pushed without having so much taken out of them as in their earlier marches. Everyone was now saddle-hardened and knew how to conserve his energies and strength. It was one o'clock on a dark cloudless Punjab winter night when they rode into Sir Harry Smith's camp; it was the 20th of January and they were ordered to be ready to march again at midnight. This gave them ample time to rest and prepare the horses.

Sir Harry Smith now had a force that consisted of a brigade each of infantry and cavalry backed by eighteen guns. He intended to march to Jagraon and open communication with

Basseen, nine miles away, along the line that was to be covered by the enormous British battering train, with its precious guns, ammunition, stores and treasure. Spread out, and moving slowly over a ten-mile stretch of ill-kept roads, this column was threatened by Runjoor Singh's army of about 10,000 men and forty guns now thought to be in position at Baranhara, seven miles from Ludhiana. When he arrived at Jagraon Sir Harry was told that the Sikhs were still at Baranhara and that they had also occupied two forts – one at Badowal and another, the strong Gungrana, ten miles from Badowal on Sir Harry's right. The force was joined by the 53rd Foot Regiment who had come over from Basseen and they all bivouacked in the open space around the fort.

The fort at Jagraon was the same as the others the troops had seen – grey mud walls with a watchtower and small huts dotted around the area outside the fort, perfectly defensible providing that the enemy did not possess any artillery. Reassuringly large and dully gleaming eighteen guns stood in their accurately lined park, limber horses tethered behind the guns; the lancers were next to them – about 530 strong – then came the Native Light Cavalry and the regiment of Irregular Horse in their colourful but practical dress. The two regiments of British infantry, the 31st and 53rd, were trying to get some rest, with their scarlet jackets on the ground by their side, for them the hardest part of all as they trudged over the heavy sandy ground in their completely unsuitable outfits. Busily cooking themselves a meal were two numerically weak regiments of native infantry, the 24th and 47th; each man using his own fire and utensils according to his religious beliefs. The hot sun and the long march had weeded out the fit from the unfit and Sir Harry was burdened by about 250 convalescents, mainly natives but with some Europeans among them.[1] The whole force of effectives totalled about 2500 infantry, 1300 cavalry and eighteen guns. Of this number, Sir Harry left two companies of native infantry and the convalescents, together with all wheeled transport and baggage, within the protection of the fort. Before leaving Jagraon Sir Harry wrote out his order of march with details of baggage guards, and read the instructions to all officers during a conference on the afternoon of the 20th. At two-hourly intervals riders were despatched to Colonel Godby at Ludhiana, ordering him to meet Sir Harry with his 'force of 4 Horse Artillery guns, a strong Regiment of Native Cavalry and four good and fresh Regiments of Native Infantry'. At half past twelve, as soon as the moon was up, he marched out of Ludhiana, intending to march by the shortest and most direct route, leaving Badowal on his right.

With the enemy at Baranhara, thirty miles from him but only seven miles from Ludhiana, Sir Harry decided not to move by the interior line between the two enemy fortresses of Gungrana and Badowal. This was a wise precaution because they were only about four miles from each of his flanks and could subject his march to double interruptions. The night was cold and clear; little moonlight, but enough light for the regiments to keep contact. They could also be kept in sight by the cavalry who rode out on their flanks, in addition to acting as a forward advance guard and a rearguard which also had the job of urging on any stragglers. There were few of these, night marching did not possess the arduousness of the weary trudge under the Punjab sun; as day dawned they were within two miles of Badowal, having covered the sixteen or eighteen miles '. . . in the most perfect order', as Sir Harry Smith wrote. There had been no signs of the enemy, although signal rockets had occasionally flared up in the distant night sky in front of them.

Just before dawn a courier from Colonel Godby arrived, bearing startling news – the Sikhs had marched away from Baranhara and were at this very moment encamped in considerable force around Badowal, close to Sir Harry's small force! This greatly changed the complexion of things; they now had two alternatives – to try to force their way boldly through by continuing on the same road, leaving Badowal on their right and, most likely, a moving Sikh army on their left; or to leave Badowal on their left and make a detour towards Gungrana. There was a third alternative open to Sir Harry Smith of retracing his steps to Jagraon and abandoning Godby, but he never seriously considered this. In view of the considerable disparity in the size of the forces Sir Harry decided that the stakes were too high to take any chances, so he ordered a change in his order of march. It was later discovered that the Sikhs had made ample preparations to meet them if they had continued on their original route, the signal rockets that they had seen during the night being used to guide a force with forty guns into an ambush position.

Soon after daybreak they halted, the cavalry rolled their cloaks and waited long enough to allow the baggage animals to get ahead; these camels were to move parallel to the troops on their right flank so as to be covered by the column. Unfortunately, in order to permit the baggage animals to use the road, the infantry were forced to plough through the fields of deep sand that stretched on either side of the road. This proved desperately tiring after the eighteen miles that they had already covered.

The column was now formed so that a single word of command would wheel them to the left into battle array; in this formation they trudged another three miles to enter the sandy plain that stretched away to Ludhiana, about six miles distant. There was still no sign of Godby and his force, but the Sikh army soon came into view on their left front about half a mile away. The enemy obviously were holding in some strength the fort of Badowal, which was on a low hill commanding the plain; their troops were also lining a long avenue of trees leading to the village of Badowal. Being in a position parallel with the British line of march, the Sikh infantry, cavalry and artillery were able to move in concert with the slow-moving column. But as they were on good roads that passed through a string of small villages, they could move faster and with less fatigue than the British and at the same time be covered by the houses.

The 16th Lancers were riding warily at the head of the column; when they came abreast of the first of the villages – not more than 300 yards from the Sikhs whom they could now pick out individually – they received their baptism of fire from the Sikh guns. A Sergeant in the leading squadron, the first to come under fire, later wrote in his diary:

'Their first shot went over our heads, and the next four rounds each killed a horse in our squadron. By taking ground to the right we were in a great measure screened from their fire by a sandbank. Their attention then seemed entirely taken up with our infantry, who were coming up – but in a most deplorable state for fighting; they were completely knocked up with the long march and many of them laid down on the sand to die.'

The unwounded troopers who had been unseated when their horses were killed, discarded their lances and equipment and began to trudge through the deep sand; they carried sword and pistol in each hand. If their situation became desperate they would be taken up behind a comrade, but at the moment a double weight on a horse was out of the question.[2] Captain Bere, the Squadron Commander, ordered them to take ground to their right so as to take advantage of the shelter offered by a low sandbank. The men sat huddled in their saddles with bowed heads, as though trying to shield themselves against rain. They acutely realised their helplessness; unless they were actually ordered to charge the enemy guns they had no means whatsoever of retaliating; they had to sit and take whatever came their way.

The fire from the Sikh guns began to slacken; the enemy artillerymen had seen the head of the infantry column coming up and turned their fire on to them. From all along the Sikh line came a hot fire, accompanied by the heavy guns mounted on the fort firing shot and shell; the projectiles came at them with a shattering roar or bounded relentlessly off a rock to tear through the close-packed ranks, leaving a bloody lane in their wake. For some of the weary infantry this was the last straw; their exhausted state made many of them completely unfit for fighting and some of the more faint-hearted after receiving only a slight wound would lay down in the sand to die.

Because of the better roads, the Sikhs were able to outdistance the tired column so that they could quickly bring into action a large number of horse-guns to flay the wearily moving column. Sir Harry Smith ordered the cavalry and horse artillery in line and between the infantry and the enemy; this move kept the Sikh cavalry off them. There was still some way to go before they finally passed the last of the villages and the horsemen had to take a considerable number of shells before they came to the partial screen formed by a low ridge of sandhills. The infantry were almost done up and could scarcely stumble along; some of them sidled alongside the cavalrymen and helped themselves along by grasping the stirrups. The idea took root and soon there was not a single horse without its attendant, shambling red-coated infantryman. Captain Bere noticed this and sent N.C.O.s galloping along the column, bawling out harshly but not unkindly:

'Come along now! Make them men leggo yer stirrups! Sorry, mate, but we can't 'ave yer 'anging on like that, can we? Say we 'ave to charge the Sixes? Where'jer be then . . . ? Come on now!'

The troopers reluctantly pushed away with spurred boots the desperate clutching fingers of the tired foot-soldiers, who resignedly dropped behind to plod on in their wake. In the meantime the eighteen guns of the Bengal Horse Artillery were moving along in the rear of the cavalry, keeping close together in their rattling, jingling progress. Soon the opportunity for which they were looking arrived; with a clatter of harness and thud of hooves they wheeled into position; the gunners leapt off the guns and limbers. Rapidly the guns were laid after being unlimbered at lightning speed, and destructive and accurate fire opened up on the Sikhs. Before the Sikh artillerymen could lay on them and return the fire they had limbered up and swung out of the position. Moving on, they would seek another similar opportunity and then repeat the impressive performance. On each occasion they would be loudly cheered by the cavalry and infantry, much in the manner of a crowd at a sporting event.

Clouds of white-robed Sikh cavalry were milling around throughout; they would dart in and out threateningly but without ever actually coming into contact with the British troops. Each time the enemy horsemen moved towards them the 16th would settle themselves in their saddles, lower their lancer points and pray for the order to charge. But Brigadier Cureton was too old a hand to fall for such tricks; keeping his cavalry tightly under control he was handling them in masterly fashion. He was restraining them from getting out of position so that the tired infantry were left without cover. He moved his regiments squadron by squadron in mutual covering manoeuvres so that the Sikh cavalry were never given the chance of getting at the infantry or any bunch of troops in overwhelming force. Instead, he would use the artillery to fire off a dozen rounds or so whenever the enemy cavalry came in close; it was a measure that went a long way towards relieving the feelings of his own horsemen. They found it heartening to see other cavalry taking what they had been getting for the past hour and not taking it in anything like the same steady fashion! The cavalrymen were disgusted at the unsportsmanlike tactics of the enemy; to them, this darting-in-and-out business seemed to be typical of foreigners.

The roundshot screamed and whistled overhead, making the short hairs bristle on the backs of their red necks. First would come the roar of the gun; they could often see it pointed at them and actually fired; then came the wailing scream of the shot. Short balls plunged and ricocheted over the rocky, sandy ground; it was not hard to visualise what these vicious black balls could do to the soft flesh of man or horse. Even the wind of the shot did damage; one of the trooper's horses suddenly dropped like a stone, throwing its rider heavily to the ground; he rose shakily to his feet and looked the horse over for a wound but could find nothing. In fury and desperation he gave the animal a nudge with his foot; immediately it shook its head and scrambled to its feet as if nothing had happened – the wind of a near miss had evidently stunned the horse. A few minutes later an officer in No. 2 Squadron was knocked off his horse by a similar wind;

within a few minutes his face was puffed and blackened with bruises as though he had been in a fight.

Whilst the majority of the Sikh artillery fire was played upon the marching column of troops, some of it ricocheted and screamed through the ranks and into the baggage camels. This caused the frightened native drivers to abandon their animals, who ran away and were plundered by hostile villagers.[3]

Quartermaster Cornes of Her Majesty's 53rd Regiment of Foot, with a party of one sergeant and thirty men were in the rearguard, in charge of the regimental baggage, but found that a party of Sikh cavalry had got between them and the main body. Some of the rearmost lancers, seeing his plight, turned and went back to assist the small party who had now been joined by some sepoys who had also become detached. In their turn the lancers found that they had been cut off, and the party, now numbering two officers and eighty men decided to fight it out and try to make their way back to Jagraon with the baggage. This was managed with but a small loss of baggage in spite of the attentions of about a thousand Sikhs with a field-gun who constantly threatened to attack but were prevented from doing so by the steady discipline of Cornes' little party. Many stragglers and sick men in the rear of the column were cut off and killed or captured, the 53rd Foot suffered particularly in this respect.[4]

The Sikh artillery fire upon the moving column was very furious, particularly upon the rear of the infantry; it was only lessened on the occasions when the horse artillery were able to reply. At one point they had the opportunity of doing this for ten minutes and the whole force of eighteen guns poured a continuous fire into the enemy ranks, doing great damage. Nevertheless, the Sikhs were being handled with exceptional skill by their commander, who, with great dexterity and speed, formed directly across the British rear a line of seven of his infantry battalions, with guns in their intervals, apparently intending to attack the British column with his line. Sir Harry Smith later said that this was '. . . a very able and well executed move, which rendered my position critical and demanded nerve and decision to avoid the coming storm'. Indeed, the fiery Sir Harry would have loved to pick up the gauntlet flung at his feet and to have gone into action by attacking the Sikh line. He was deeply tempted to do so and, in fact, formed up the 31st Foot for the attack, but so deep was the sand and so fatigued were the men that he was compelled to abandon the project. By now the infantry had marched nearly twenty miles in nine hours in deep, clogging sand and a charge might be equally fatal to the exhausted victors. The fierce and unquestioning discipline of the British troops showed its worth here as Sir Harry Smith ordered his men to carry out a manoeuvre which is considered difficult even on a parade ground – he changed front on the centre of the 31st Regiment and of the 53rd, a counter-march on the centre by wings: '. . . the move was executed as accurately as at a review; then became conspicuous the majesty of discipline and bravery', later wrote Sir Harry.

This sense of bravery and discipline, encouraged by the confidence and example of Sir Harry Smith, was to be the main factor in getting them out of trouble. The native regiments remained steady, and the whole of the infantry were now directed to march to Ludhiana in echelon of battalions, ready to receive the word 'Halt front' when they could thus confront the enemy's line if he advanced. The cavalry were re-formed so as to move in echelon of squadrons, the two arms mutually supporting; the guns were in rear of the cavalry. Sir Harry was delighted with the way in which his orders were obeyed in the most correct and steady manner. Apparently the Sikhs were equally impressed, because, notwithstanding their overwhelming force, they did not attack nor attempt to get too far away from their Badowal stronghold.[5]

Brigadier Cureton handled the three regiments of cavalry most skilfully, the lancers particularly feeling that they were learning the facts of life very quickly under this vital cavalry commander. Their dispositions covered the movement of the exhausted column, protected stragglers and prevented them from falling into the enemy hands. The day had been intensely hot, and the fatigue of the sorely tried infantry was so great that many of them had collapsed. Without orders the cavalry had picked up their unconscious bodies and draped them across their saddle-fronts, whilst others dragged one foot painfully in front of the other as they clung to the stirrup leathers.

In spite of having been in the saddle for sixteen hours, the men were exhilarated at their first action under fire. It had served an admirable purpose in that it had accustomed them to the scream of shot and shell without causing them heavy casualities; in all the lancers only lost two killed and one wounded. In the infantry regiments men were sick and disheartened, nearly 400 of whom were missing at the end of the march, but more than 200 of them straggled in during the next twelve hours.[6]

One squadron of the 16th Lancers were ordered to go back and cover the stragglers who were being slaughtered and captured by the Sikh cavalry. The Squadron Commander turned and went back at the gallop, the men putting spurs to their mounts and following close behind him. They passed those infantrymen who were walking, reeling and shambling a little behind their regiments; the cavalrymen looked down pityingly into their bearded, dusty faces ribboned with rivers of sweat running down from their white-covered shakoes, appealing and desperate eyes looked back at them. The Sikhs began to shout and wave their weapons when they saw them turn back, but did not move towards them. Each lancer sought a stumbling, reeling red-coated figure or else a bundle of scarlet and blue rags lying face down in the sand. Those men who could still walk clung to their stirrup leathers and irons; those who were unconscious they dragged painfully to their feet and bundled them across the front of the saddle like a sack of oats. Laboriously and un-military, but strangely awe-inspiring the laden horsemen made their slow way back towards the creeping red caterpillar that wound ahead of them. Frequently turning to face the Sikhs in case they took their chance to attack, the lancers walked back over the dusty, shot-torn ground, their fatigued horses each dragging or carrying a combined weight of about forty stone.

11

Chasing the Sikhs

It was a tired and miserable force that drifted into Ludhiana. They were greeted by the small garrison and by Godby's force which had also just arrived. Sir Harry ordered them to combine in a guarded camp in front of the town, then, too tired for food, the exhausted men sank in the tracks and slept. When the men awoke they were stiff, sick and disheartened; they looked around them and assessed their losses – there seemed to be some big gaps in the ranks.[1] The other ranks of the 16th Lancers heard that their hospital stores and officers' mess-kit had been lost; perversely, they found the news strangely funny and soon gusts of laughter from their area caused other men to look strangely across at them.

There was not much rest for the cavalry, who were ordered out on picquet almost immediately, but they did not find this unpleasant; they were out of the way of strict discipline of an unreasoning nature and worked in small groups under a sergeant. They were out in the pleasant early-morning freshness of the Punjab winter, were warmed by the hotter hours in the middle of the day and they enjoyed the cool evenings. Sir Harry Smith would have liked to establish himself nearer to the enemy, but lack of a suitable position with adequate water prevented this. He noted that the Sikhs were obviously disinclined to leave the shelter of the villages, fearing to encounter in the open the now united British force. So he established his outposts close upon them, using his cavalry unsparingly in constant patrols right up to the Sikh positions; he was watching, waiting and anticipating an opportunity to redeem the somewhat ignominious loss of his baggage!

Brigadier Cureton carefully ensured that there were always native cavalry or irregular cavalry with each British patrol; in this way they were groomed and taught the job so that each man felt that he was learning his trade under master hands and in the company of veterans at the game. But every man still longed for the chance to show, in a full-blooded charge, just what he could do!

As dawn broke on the 22nd of January, a cavalry patrol eased themselves in their saddles and gazed through the slight mist that heralded the coming of daylight. Looming ahead of them, they could see the shadow of the grey-mud-walled fort and the few low houses of the village of Badowal. Within a few minutes they knew they would be able to discern the Sikh soldiers moving about; then they would receive their usual morning salutation of a few rounds of shot from the enemy guns, screaming overhead and burying themselves harmlessly in the sandy ground. It became lighter, the buildings became larger and blacker; but the morning guns were late and there seemed to be little sign of life about the place. Then, suddenly, it was fully light; Badowal and its environments stood fully revealed in the brightening sunlight; there were still no signs of life. Cautiously, the patrol moved forward until they were within a hundred yards of the buildings; nothing happened, no guns fired or muskets rattled. Emboldened, they rode warily forward until the advance earthworks were reached; they sat on their horses peering up at the mud walls of the fort towering twenty feet above them.

The place was completely deserted; the Sikhs had abandoned it silently during the night. A courier was sent back to inform Sir Harry and the rest of the patrol entered the village. The Sikhs had left nothing of value except some grain and a few stores; there were also some of the less useful items plundered from the captured British baggage. Forward came a regiment of infantry, at the double, as Sir Harry rushed to put the village in a state of defence.[2] The British commander was bristling with eagerness to get at the Sikhs; he knew that he was in a good position and that Runjoor Singh had missed his chance by not attacking the weary column during the Badowal march. Now the Sikh commander had the British across his line of communication with Phillaur and was compelled to rely on a ford further down the River Sutlej as his line of retreat. Although he was still awaiting final reinforcements coming up under the command of Brigadier Wheeler, Sir Harry felt that he had enough men to attack the Sikhs if he could catch them on the march or out of strong entrenchments.[3]

The British force lay for four days awaiting Wheeler's reinforcements; Sir Harry was kept informed of the enemy's movements by Cureton's cavalry patrols, who were closely watching Runjoor Singh as he moved towards the Vallore Hills, flanking the direct road from Ludhiana to Ferozepor. On the 26th of January Wheeler's force marched in, dead tired.[4] They were allowed to rest through the day of the 27th, while the remainder of Smith's men prepared for the battle they hoped to force on the Sikhs next day. Godby, who had been left in command at Ludhiana when the main force moved forward to Badowal, rode into camp with his men. He had left Ludhiana guarded by the invalids and a small force. Sir Harry now had a total strength of 12,000 men with thirty-two guns, a force he considered quite adequate to defeat the slightly larger Sikh army.[5]

At first light on the 28th of January 1846, proudly headed by small, dark Sir Harry Smith on his spirited Arabian charger, the force marched out to the north-west. They were led by the cavalry, in contiguous columns to squadrons of regiments, with two batteries of horse artillery in the intervals between brigades. In the rear of the horse marched the infantry, also in contiguous columns of brigades, at intervals of deploying distance; the open spaces were filled by artillery. With the idea of looking for any hostile movement towards Badowal or Ludhiana a native cavalry regiment were sent wide to the eastward.

They had been marching for two hours or so when a small cloud of dust indicated the arrival of a rider; it was a ragged native scout who was immediately taken to Sir Harry Smith. After a brief conversation Sir Harry sent gallopers down the column to summon his brigade commanders; the assembled order group were told that his spy had reported the Sikh army to be out in the open! It seemed that they were moving on Jagraon with the apparent intention of occupying it and relieving the Gungrana fort – two posts that were very close to the line of British communications with the Jumna. Rumours and whispers ran up and down the column; like a pack of hounds who had scented the fox, the nostrils of every soldier in the force twitched at the thought of bringing the enemy to battle outside entrenchments. The march assumed a new and refreshing aspect; straps were tightened, packs were adjusted, muskets were inspected and steps were lighter – the chase was on! When the brigade commanders returned and gave their orders the news spread through the ranks like a rippling fire; the men gave a spontaneous cheer that was rigorously suppressed by the sergeants and officers. The men were instructed to look to their caps and primings; this brought tingling to the senses – it was a sure sign that action was impending.

In spite of the increasing heat of the day they went forward light-heartedly, their feet seemed to come up from the sandy soil much faster than before and the five miles over the rough ground passed quickly. The head of the column reached the top of a sandy ridge crowned by a small, tumbledown village which did not seem to be inhabited, the grey mud walls were crumbling and the roofs gaped open to the sky. Maps were hastily opened and studied; it seemed that the village was Poorain. The column was halted. Sir Harry and a group of staff officers clambered on to the roof of what seemed to be the safest of the ramshackle houses. Whilst they were laboriously climbing up, a cavalry scout of the 16th Lancers galloped up:

'Compliments o' Brigadier Cureton, sir! Enemy reported in sight directly ahead!'

Sir Harry Smith's bright blue eyes lit up, he could hardly contain his excitement; he acknowledged the message and clambered on to the flat roof of the house. He swept his eyes round the horizon that lay spread out before him; at the foot of the ridge on which they were perched lay a level plain some two miles long and one mile wide. Beyond, at the furthest edge of the plain, was a gentle rise on which were two villages; maps were again consulted and Sir Harry was told that the village on his right was Aliwal and that on his left was Bhundri. The latter was masked by a thin grove of trees and was not in any apparent defensive state, while Aliwal appeared to be fortified by earthen breastworks which also ran in a curved line along the ridge and connected the two places. These waist-high earthen banks gave the impression that the Sikhs had halted for the night and thrown up rudimentary fortifications in case of attack; through the glasses it was possible to detect some heavy guns still in position. At the back of the position the river gleamed in the bright sunlight; between it and the ridge lay the Sikh encampment – the tents were being struck and men could be seen bustling around the area like flies.

The Sikhs had just begun to march out in the direction of Jagraon; they were spread in a straggling column, the end of which was still emerging from the camp like a snake from a basket. Seeing the British, the column halted, realising that they might well be taken in flank. In the manner of ants when a stick stirs their ant-hill they rushed in all directions back to the villages and the entrenchments, which they hastily occupied. Through the glass they could be seen frantically trying to raise the height of the earthworks and to pile banks of soil in front of the guns.

Sir Harry gave a long low whistle through his teeth:

'By God! There they are! Now I've got them!'

Raising his glass, he carefully studied the whole area, slowly moving it across the terrain from one side to the other in a slow and methodic manner. Now and then he would lower it and gaze out through half-closed lids as he feverishly worked out his troop dispositions and his course of action; without taking his gaze from the arena spread in front of him, he exchanged over his shoulder an occasional word with one staff officer or another. In the clear dustless air of the bright sunlit morning the battle-ground lay open like a theatre set; there was a fine grassy plain with the mud villages standing up on either flank; in the rear the river gleamed – it gave the appearance of a carefully laid-out toy model. But no toymaker could simulate the unique natural backdrop; in their majesty and beauty the snowy ranges of the Himalayas formed an unsurpassed background. Beautiful as the picture undoubtedly was, it escaped Sir Harry's eyes in these circumstances. Suddenly, he swung characteristically round and began to clamber briskly to the ground, followed by a milling crowd of officers all seeking to be first on the ground with their beloved commander.

12

The Battle of Aliwal

Sir Harry Smith in his whole life had never wanted anything so much as he desired to fight and beat this Sikh army that had given him so much trouble a few days before. He wanted to beat them without losing the large numbers of men who had fallen in the earlier battles of Mudki and Ferozeshah. But, above all, he wanted to prove both to himself and his men that there were more skilful ways of winning battles than by throwing the soft, even if willing, flesh of British soldiers against entrenched heavy guns.

'Well, I fancy that the key to the situation is that village of Aliwal! It's not as strongly held as the other one, Bhundri. We'll make Aliwal our first objective!'

He turned to Brigadier Cureton, who had galloped up:

'Charlie, we've got them, don't you think? Now, do you take your cavalry and deploy right and left. McDowell's brigade on the left and Stedman's on the right. Or do you prefer to change them?'

By bringing up his right flank and carrying Aliwal, which was in front of the Sikh left, Sir Harry reasoned that he could throw himself with great effect upon their left and centre, so cutting off their line of retreat by the fords over the river. He felt sure that the Sikhs had made a grave tactical error by accepting battle with a river in their rear; their left flank was actually on the banks of the Sutlej. He felt a glow of satisfaction that his swift moves of that morning had hardly given them the option of any other course of action. He gazed again through his glass, noting that the Sikhs were positioned along the crest of rising ground, their guns placed all along the front of their line, which was facing south-east.

It was now ten o'clock, the sun shone brightly on the hard open grassland from which no dust arose. The scene was striking as the British force, facing north-west, began to move steadily and impressively forward. Now begins the actual battle story, with all the pomp and pageantry of an old-time army in its full dress; it was to be a battle in the last of the wars of the British Army still remembered like Waterloo and the Peninsular. They went into action with an Order of Battle that really was an Order of Battle and caused the troops to form up and fight accordingly; each unit was in line of column, the cavalry were on the flanks and the artillery were in the intervals – all under the command of men who were veterans of the Peninsular War of forty years earlier. Nor had the uniform and accoutrements changed a great deal since Waterloo in 1815; the Sikh War was fought in the relatively cold climate of a northern Indian winter and the Army wore the old-style European dress.[1]

The British array moved down the slope upon which stood Poorain and reached the firm, grassy ground at its foot. Brigadier Cureton have orders for the cavalry to deploy; the horsemen opened their glittering ranks and wheeled off to each flank. The 1st Brigade, under Brigadier McDowell,[2] formed of the 16th Lancers, the 3rd Light Cavalry and the 4th Irregular Cavalry, went to the left. Peeling off right went the 2nd Brigade under Brigadier Stedman; it was formed of the Governor-General's Bodyguard, the 1st and 5th Native Cavalry and Major Foster's Shekawati Cavalry. The jogging horsemen were a colourful picture as they moved easily, rhythmically, forward – the 16th Lancers in scarlet with pennons, per fesse red and white, lightly fluttering from the lances; the Irregular Horse in dark blue and gold, and the native cavalry in their silver-grey trimmed with scarlet.

His front cleared, Sir Harry Smith now began to deploy his infantry who for the first time saw the whole Sikh force now drawn up on the rising ground, their cavalry in front. He placed two infantry brigades in the front rank – Wheeler's (H.M.'s 50th Regiment, the 48th Native Infantry and the Sirmoor Gurkhas) on the right; Wilson's brigade (H.M.'s 53rd Regiment, the 30th Native Infantry and the Shekawati Brigade) on the left. Echeloned in rear of them were Godby's brigade (the Gurkhas of the Nusseree Battalion and the 47th Native Infantry) on the right, and Hicks' brigade (H.M.'s 31st Regiment and the 24th and 36th Native Infantry) on the left. In this order Sir Harry Smith advanced as though on parade, every manoeuvre executed perfectly, with the 12,000 men acting as one – rarely has there been a more stately prelude to a general action.

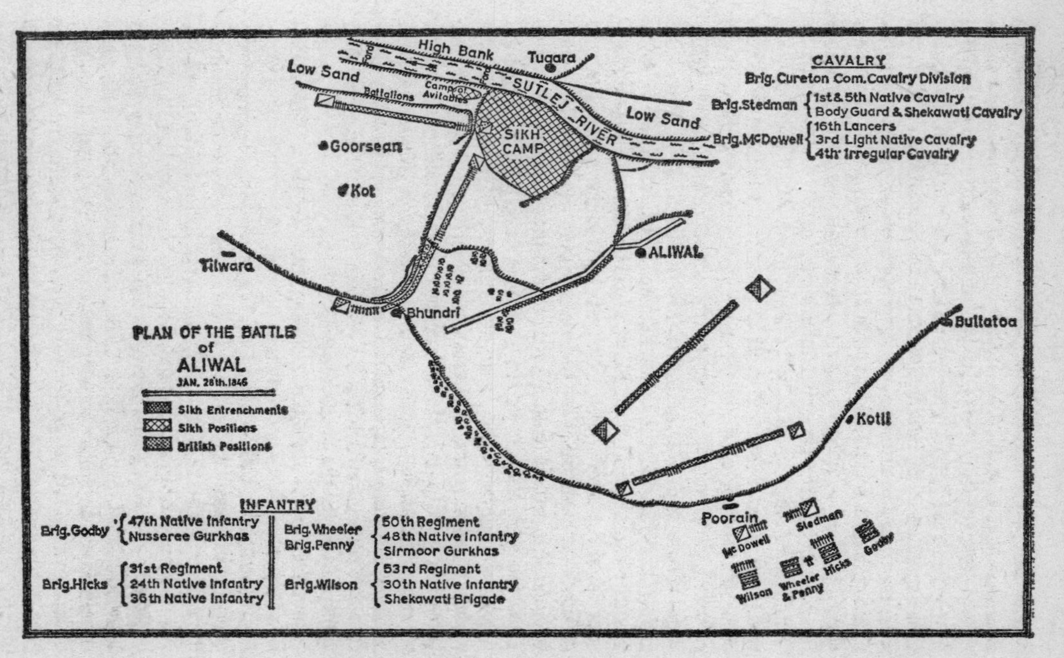

The Battle of Aliwal January 28th, 1846

Suddenly a spontaneous burst of cheering began among the British ranks; it rippled and swelled into a roar as it was taken up all along the line. This time the officers and sergeants did not try to check the sound, they waved their arms and led the 'three-times-three' that the soldiers were giving Sir Harry. The native infantry joined in and the uproar echoed on all sides; nevertheless, the native sepoys did not really understand why they were cheering; they could never quite understand this British passion for fighting and the pleasure that it aroused.

Before they had gone very far Sir Harry noticed that his army was outflanked by the Sikh left, so he wheeled his line into column, took ground to his right, once again wheeled the columns into line and continued the movement forward. When they were within 600 or 700 yards of the Sikh positions the enemy earthworks were dramatically obscured from view by clouds of smoke and the still air reverberated with the crashing roar of heavy guns. Then followed the familiar screaming wail of shot and shell; the first rounds dropped short and ploughed up the hard ground with spurts of dust that looked like water. Then the Sikh gunners began to get the range and the hurtling, whistling roundshot began to tear bloody paths through the closely ordered ranks. The grim and silently advancing infantry bent their heads forward and hunched their shoulders as though pushing against a wild gale of winter; brusquely ordered by their officers and non-commissioned officers, they closed up their ranks as each gap occurred. Sir Harry saw that the moment had arrived to begin the battle proper.

Summoning Godby's brigade from the right rear, he launched it, together with Hicks' brigade, against the village of Aliwal. As the brigades formed up, Her Majesty's 31st Regiment, the only British regiment in the two brigades, viewed the Sikh entrenchments with some misgivings, having bitter memories of the 300 men they had lost charging with the bayonet against similar positions at Mudki and Ferozeshah. Another deadly struggle seemed certain, for the Sikh ranks were steady and their guns were firing accurately and well, but the job had to be done. The orders were given to go forward and, bayonet-tipped muskets held out in front of them, the British and native infantry moved off steadily, each man with his head slightly bowed as though walking into wind-driven rain and his body, left shoulder forward, instinctively drawn in as much as possible. Advancing at a steady pace, the men began to shout and cheer; their speed increased as they got nearer to the Sikh position. The open ground made it possible for them to advance in perfect order, aided by their officers and zealous sergeants, who canstantly checked their dressing and ordered them to close up and fill the gaps. They were principally receiving grapeshot from their left and centre, but closed up the gaps within their ranks and continued the advance. Very little small-arms fire had been received and the general feeling was that the Sixes were holding their fire until the infantry were close enough for every bullet to count.

When there was only about 150 yards to go to reach the entrenchments a ragged, irregular volley ripped out from the levelled muskets of the Sikhs, whose brown faces and turbans could be clearly seen above the earth banks. A sprinkling of men fell along the line, a mere handful in comparison with what they had expected – and the experienced infantry knew that they were too close for the enemy to have time to reload and give them a second volley! Pausing only to pour in a heavy volley,[3] the cheering British and native infantry rushed over the last few yards of the level grassy ground leading to the village of Aliwal. Over the earthen banks they plunged, cheering and shouting, into the reeling Sikh infantry and the guns; their faithful gunners backed up against them defending themselves with tulwars, ramrods and reversed muskets. These were not the steady Sikh infantry of Mudki and Ferozeshah – dressed in a variety of ragged and dirty robes, the enemy infantry were battalions of hillmen with no heart for the struggle and they turned to flee. In a few minutes it was all over, and the village was in British hands; the gunners had died to a man fighting around their guns, two of which had fallen into British hands. The fleeing hillmen had been pursued to the edge of the village, being cut down and pierced through and through their backs with the bayonets of the exultant infantry. The Nusseree Gurkhas fought valiantly; casting aside their muskets after they had stormed over the parapets with their flashing, wide-bladed knives (kukris) they carved a bloody path through the frightened Sikh irregular soldiers.

Delighted by the success of his right flank, Sir Harry Smith ordered a general attack upon the Sikh centre and left. Brigadier Wheeler's 2nd Brigade, supported by Wilson, advanced to the attack and were soon heavily engaged; they took considerable punishment from fierce artillery fire. The guns of Alexander, Turton, Lane, Mill, Boileau and the Shekawati Brigade, plus two eight-inch howitzers, pushed continually out in front of the British infantry and engaged in a spirited duel with the Sikh gunners. The Horse Artillery were repeating their brilliant feats of the Badowal march; flashing repeatedly in and out, firing and then limbering up and retreating out of range before they could be hit. Nevertheless, the Sikh gunners were good and occasionally horses and gunners crashed to the ground under the hail of grapeshot and musketry that came at them from behind the earthworks.[4] The battle-field was fast becoming shrouded in the usual swirling and eddying clouds of smoke so that the British gunners had little to aim at except the flashes from the Sikh guns as they fired. The enemy's batteries being on a curve with their flanks thrown back, caused Wheeler's brigade in the centre of the British line to be nearer and more exposed to the enemy's fire than were the other brigades. But they advanced most steadily, halting twice and lying down under the fire, to steady the men and prevent undignified hurry, and to allow Wilson's brigade to get forward. The advance continued in this manner; the artillery advancing forward and opening fire, then Wheeler's brigade, with the 50th Regiment prominent, advancing up to them and laying down – this was done three times. Wheeler's brigade were exposed to a very heavy artillery fire as well as that of the musket and matchlock men. They advanced rapidly until they came close upon the Sikhs and when within effective musket range they fired a volley which caused the retreat of many of the infantry facing them, the artillerymen alone remaining fast.

Realising that his left was in serious danger of being turned, Runjoor Singh, the Sikh Commander, now tried to change his front left back, pivoting on Bhundri. To cover this movement he sent forward from that village a large body of his cavalry whilst he reorganised his position. Seeing this, Sir Harry ordered Cureton to send his own cavalry forward to attack the enemy horsemen. When the galloper came storming up to the Brigadier the 16th Lancers felt sure that they would be sent forward to see off the enemy; they looked to their horses, settled in their saddles and waited for the order. To their fury and disappointment Charlie Cureton sent the native cavalry forward; they dashed fiercely into the Sikh horsemen and quickly sent them reeling back in disorder upon their own infantry positioned in their rear.

This was the moment that Sir Harry had awaited: determined to press his advantage to the utmost, he called forward Hicks' infantry brigade to the support of the cavalry. Being now on the summit of the high ground, Sir Harry could see that the enemy's camp alongside the river was full of infantry; he sent off a galloper to order Godby's brigade to hit their left flank and rear. This move was highly successful, Godby carried everything before him – taking the opportunity of re-establishing himself in his commander's eyes after the Badowal débâcle. The rapid and successful movement of the British and native troops meant tha Runjoor Singh's force was in dire trouble, with their retreat by the river fords seriously threatened. He again tried to save himself by sending forward another large body of cavalry to cover him as he re-formed his lines at right angles to the river, by throwing back his left and using the village of Bhundri as a pivot.

Lieutenant-Colonel McDowell, commanding the 1st Cavalry Brigade, looked around him; he knew his own regiment badly wanted to go in, but feared to commit them in case they were needed for greater things later on. He made up his mind: he ordered forward a squadron of the 3rd Light Native Cavalry, supported by the 4th Squadron of the 16th Lancers under Captain Bere. The 16th were nearly in a state of mutiny; for two hours they had been sitting under the hot sun, chafing as they watched the battle unfold before their eyes. There had only been one occasion when cavalry had been required and then the native cavalry had been used. Now they saw Godby's infantry surge forward and seemingly win the battle off their own bat – it was almost more than they could bear!

This waiting was the very devil; a man felt hot and sticky and then chill and trembling in turns; the mouth was dry and the hands a little shaky. The old soldiers sat impassive, looking steadily to the front, apparently unmoved by what was going on around them; even when stray roundshot ploughed into the ground nearby they did not turn their heads. They knew that there was a comradeship in battle, that your friends were around you and would help you if trouble came your way. Some of the men were restlessly talking in low tones out of the corners of their mouths; others sat chewing their moustaches and viewing the situation with their veteran's eyes; others fairly wriggled in the saddle at the prospect and thought of action.

Sergeant Newsome moved towards his troop; he was a good type of N.C.O., with a ruddy open face framed in a measured three inches of fair whiskers besides the ears and a thin line of moustache shadowing firm lips; his eyes were lively and intelligent, with a spark of sarcastic humour playing about them. He addressed them:

'Now, look here, lads. If we goes at them Sixes don't any of you feel frit. Just you put your horses at 'em and go with the rest of the reg'ment. We're all together and we'll all see that no one comes to any harm!'

Some of the younger soldiers stared at him in amazement; tears started in one or two eyes; never had they had such words of understanding and compassion from a superior officer; they nodded their heads. Everyone sat straighter in the saddle, gripped tightly the sticky shaft of the lance, took a firmer grip of the rein and made up their minds that they were going to glorious deeds. The men saw Colonel McDowell wave his hand at them and at the squadron of the 3rd Light Native Cavalry alongside them; this was it – now they were to go! A whisper rippled through the ranks:

'Here it is, boys! We're a-going!'

Captain Bere looked across at the commander of the light cavalry, seeking confirmation that they were to go together. But the light cavalry did not seem to have understood the order; they made no attempt to move, nor did they look prepared to do so. Captain Bere had been chewing his moustache impatiently for the past two hours and he had no intention of being done out of action now that the chance had appeared. He stood up in his stirrups, turned to face his squadron and roared above the noise of battle:

'No. 4 Squadron 16th Lancers! The squadron will advance! Walk! March! Trot!'

He was completely confident that he was doing the right thing in going forward alone. He knew that the 16th Lancers were among the finest light cavalry in the world; that they were drilled and disciplined to perfection; bold by nature and filled with British self-confidence he felt with them that the time had come to put on a show before the veterans of Mudki and Ferozeshah.

The troop officers and N.C.O.s dressed and re-dressed their lines as they moved slowly forward; it seemed to take an unendurable time. Sergeant Newsome leaned across to Sergeant Gould:

'Gawd, Ben! Old Bere's going to charge that bloody great mob of Sixes with only sixty of us . . . an' we're charging uphill at that!'

The squadron moved easily forward, dressing as they came; the unhurried and extraordinary deliberation displayed by the small group of cavalry seemed to affect the morale of the Sikh cavalry. The huge mass of white-robed horsemen came to a lingering halt; they sat watching the British horsemen whilst their commanders raggedly threw out two wings with the object of outflanking Captain Bere; it was elementary cavalry tactics to be on the move when receiving a charge – cavalry who receive a charge when halted sustain a far greater shock than when they are in motion. This was an opportunity too good to be missed – he ordered his trumpeter to sound the 'Charge!' The brassy, brazen notes rang out to stir the blood and inflame the minds of the jogging troopers of No. 4 Squadron.

Five hundred yards away was the huge Sikh cavalry mass, white-robed with gaily coloured turbans, and the sun gleaming on drawn tulwars, spears and the closely woven chainmail worn by some of the officers. They were drawn up in such a dense group, with two wings far outflanking and enclosing Bere's little force, waiting to squeeze and crush, like the tentacles of an octopus. Bere, his trumpeter immediately behind him, had drawn his sword, and, looking straight ahead, led his small force headlong, stirrup to stirrup, up the slope. Suddenly, almost surprisingly, they crashed furiously into the Sikh mass. First Bere and his trumpeter and then the whole line were swallowed up, lost and engulfed in the great white Sikh mass; then suddenly they became again visible as bright specks of scarlet, like blood flecking the Sikh white robes, fighting, their lances moving in and out, their sword-arms moving like toys. The great Sikh mass began to heave, to sway, to surge this way and that, the two wings began to wheel inward to cut off the handful of British cavalry. It was an engagement of dozens of hand-to-hand fights, pistols and carbines or muskets were not used; men stabbed, hacked and chopped at each other, cursing ceaselessly; when their weapons broke or were torn from their hands, they tore at each other with fingernails. Over the sullen roar of the battle that was going in around them could be heard the sharp clatter of sword upon sword, punctuated by wild yells and screams as the Sikh mass, heaving, surging, swayed this way and that. So tightly locked was it that men found themselves paralysed by dead bodies of their enemies falling across their saddles and into their arms. Then came a new sound, that of British cheers, the mêlée was no longer surging to and fro, but swaying in one direction – uphill. The Sikhs were being pushed back! They gave a gigantic heave, swayed, rocked and suddenly spawned forth on their far side the scarlet coats of the remaining 16th Lancers, as though they had just emerged from the womb of the violently struggling white carpet. The Sikh cavalry were now in full flight, streaming away towards the river, being hunted by cheering lancers bent on killing as many of the enemy as possible.

To the men of No. 4 Squadron, who made the charge, it all seemed a crowded noisy nightmare without a beginning or an end. Suddenly they had found themselves tightly jammed on all sides by bearded, fierce-visaged brown men; occasionally the kaleidoscope was flecked with a splash of scarlet as a lancer momentarily showed. They could hardly move their arms because of the crowding; and the Sikhs sat semi-lifeless as though stunned by the audacity of the attack – allowing themselves to be shunted back and forth as though moving towards an indeterminate destination. After it was over, few of the Lancers could recall definitely striking a blow, but all knew that they had done so because their lance pennons had turned into soggy red streamers that clung stickily to the top of the shafts. It all seemed too impersonal for a man to feel afraid or to even have time to feel fear. Then, as suddenly as they had entered the mass, they were out of it; they found themselves free of the confining, surging bodies that had been around them but were now streaming away towards the river. Some of the Sikhs and indeed some of the 16th Lancers were reeling in their saddles, clutching their horses' manes; others dropped lifelessly from their horses and were dragged bumpingly along as their foot remained fixed in the stirrup. Some of the lancers set off in pursuit of the fleeing Sikhs, who turned their heads to look over the shoulder in horror at the stained lance points stretching out threateningly at their backs. The lancers spurred their horses forward, lowered the point of the lance and bunched their bodies ready to take the shock of impact – just as they had been taught to do so at Hounslow. Aiming the point directly below the coloured patches that bedecked the white robes, the men found that sometimes the lance did not penetrate easily through striking the vertebral column, but then it would slip to one side and slide into the white robe. The unfortunate Sikh would arch forward at the impact and then slump in the saddle, the weight of his lifeless body nearly tearing the lance from the grasp of its bearer, who would desperately turn the lance to loosen the head and then drag it free.

Thoughts of pursuit and frenzied excitement were momentarily driven from their mind by the repeated strident call of the trumpet, backed by Captain Bere's hoarse voice. Both were frantically endeavouring to re-form the squadron and get them under control once again. Within a few minutes most of them had re-grouped in a jubilant panting bunch, all shouting, laughing and demonstrating excitedly. Even their horses had caught the spirit and were wheeling and cavorting as though relating to each other their recent exploits. Losses seemed amazingly light, there seemed to be as many present as when they started; one man had a Sikh turban on his lance point and was waving it like a banner, another was pushing his lance point into the ground to clean it; others, old feuds forgotten, were noisily congratulating each other on some mutual passage of arms. Sergeant Newsome was circling the group trying to re-form them into some recognised order; Captain Bere intended returning to his own lines for further orders.

Finally they moved off, walking their horses through the drifting smoke; small, menacing groups of enemy infantry or cavalry were skirted; occasionally they were fired upon from one or other of their flanks. The party got the impression that they were a detached part of the battle; they could hear it going on all around them but could see little owing to the dense clouds of smoke that hung motionless in the windless air. They moved in what they felt was the direction from which they had come, hoping that they would hit by chance the rest of the cavalry brigades. Out of the smoke loomed the shapeless mass of a gun-team that had caught the full blast of grape from a Sikh battery; the horses lay draped across the pole of the limber; the gunners were all dead; some had their legs trapped beneath the carcasses of the horses, others huddled on the limber seats. The squadron altered their course to skirt the obstacle.

The change of direction brought them face to face through the smoke with a large force of Sikh infantry. Both groups halted and surveyed each other at less than a hundred yards' distance; training and discipline asserted themselves and both took immediate action. These Sikhs were not the low-moraled irregulars who had fled from Aliwal village, but crack 'Aieen' infantry trained by a French mercenary General Avitabile. They showed the benefit of their European training by calmly forming themselves into an irregular square in preparation for the cavalry attack. The lancers settled themselves in the saddle, tightly grasped their lances, lowered their points and prepared to charge. Captain Bere raised his sword, stood in his stirrups and pointed at the enemy:

'Squadron! Form line! Gallop! Charge!'

The trumpeter sounded the charge over and over again; men, hoarse with shouting, found voice enough to raise a cheer and the squadron hurtled forward. In the short time it took to cover the ground between them the Sikh infantry got off a ragged volley and emptied a few saddles at close range – and then the lancers were into them! The sheer weight of the charge smashed their formation into disorder; the squadron hit the infantry with an audible thud, the horses perceptibly pausing at the impact which sent the infantry reeling in all directions. But the discipline of the Sikhs came to their rescue; they threw away their empty muskets and drew curved swords with which they defended themselves. Some of them had large round shields slung on their backs which they quickly brought into use.[5]

The cavalry went straight through and emerged into the open on the other side of the now shattered Sikh square; they were just in time to see Captain Fyler's squadron ride through another Sikh formation about sixty yards to one side of them. The two squadrons combined and rode back to their own lines; the 3rd British Infantry Brigade with two guns had come up to complete the rout in that area.

Captain E. B. Bere had received a facial wound and was a fearsome sight; capless and with one side of his face as scarlet as his tunic, the blood dripping from the ends of his short beard and down on to his chest. He did not appear to notice his wound and continued to order and encourage his squadron as he had done throughout the conflict. Just after the two squadrons joined, Captain Fyler reeled and fell from his saddle, having been struck in the thigh by a cannon-ball from one of the zumburrucks (camel-swivel guns mounted on camel-back and firing a small one-pound cannon-ball). So Captain Bere, wound and all, became commander of the two squadrons.

They found the regiment suddenly coming upon them through the haze; they took their places to the sound of cheers from all sides. Officers rode over and congratulated Captain Bere; troopers leaned across and called out eager questions; envy showed on the faces of those who had not had the good fortune to take part in the charges. Throughout the action the cavalry were in reserve but under heavy fire, a Sikh battery directly to their front galling them with a continual and destructive hail. The shot whistled about their ears, ploughed huge furrows in the ground and small pieces of metal ricocheted in all directions, often sinking with a dull thud into the bodies of the horses.

Brigadier Wilson was ordered to charge this battery with his infantry brigade (H.M.'s 53rd Foot, the Shekawati and the 30th Native Infantry). The orders rang out and the men moved forward with heads bowed, bodies hunched forward and bayonets glittering from the muskets held in front of their bodies. Brigadier

Cureton followed with keen interest the progress of this infantry attack, awaiting the precise moment to launch his eager horsemen into the attack. He noted that the infantry were suffering heavy losses and that the 30th Native Infantry were beginning to waver, losing their place in line with the other two regiments of the brigade; but Charlie Cureton judged that it was not yet the time to move.[6] The cavalry force stood their ground; their horses were restless under the continual fire and the noise and were being controlled with difficulty. On all sides men were dropping from their horses on to the hard-baked ground with jingling crashes; horses were sinking to their knees silently or setting the teeth on edge with piteous neighing. Above the distant cheers, the groans, the hiss and ping of balls passing around them the cavalry responded to the words of command that cut through the din.

'Close in on your centre, men!'

'Get back, the right flank!'

'Keep up, Private Collins!'

'Left squadron, get back, look to your dressing!'

'Close in! Close in! Close in!'

Then Cureton saw his chance: he whirled round in his saddle and sent his galloper dashing through the smoke to Major Rowland Smyth, commander of the 16th Lancers. Smyth rapped out a sharp order to his trumpeter; the shrill notes rang above the chaos and set the regiment off at the trot with a jangling and a creaking. Major Smyth rode alone some lengths in front, with his trumpeter behind him; it was the greatest day of his life; he was equipped with great physical courage and supremely well suited to command his regiment in action. At first he rode quietly at the trot, stiff and upright in the saddle, never looking back; he well knew that a cavalry commander leading a charge must always keep his gaze strictly forward lest his men riding behind feel that he is uncertain of them. In perfect order the regiment moved forward under heavy fire which caused them to instinctively increase their pace; it was a natural inclination to gallop forward as fast as their horses would carry them so that they could get to grips with the enemy and out of this harassing fire. But their pace was tightly restrained by Major Smyth; he was determined that they should advance with parade-ground precision and perfection. When Captain Pearson shot up level with Major Smyth, he was instantly checked by the Major's sword laid across his chest;[7] without turning his head, Major Smyth growled at his subordinate:

'Captain Pearson! You are not to force the pace! You do not

ride level with your commanding officer!' Then his voice rose above the clamour: 'Steady, steady, the 16th!' He rose in his stirrups, turned to face them; raised his voice to a roar: 'Now! I am going to give the order to charge! Three cheers for the Queen!'

There was a terrific burst of cheering in reply and the men settled down to the hurtling, headlong, stirrup-to-stirrup dash over the last couple of hundred yards. The lancers were meeting death in perfect order; as a man or a horse dropped, the riders on each side of him opened out; as soon as they had ridden clear, the ranks closed again. Orderly as if on parade, the lancers rode on, their numbers being depleted; what the regular mechanical movements meant in terms of discipline and courage was unaccountable. As the casualties became heavier, the squadrons could not keep their entity, formation was lost and the front line broke into a mad gallop. The men could no longer be restrained and began to shoot forward in front of their officers, who were forced to increase their pace or be overwhelmed. The gallop became headlong, the men cheering and shouting, their blood was up and they were on fire to get at the enemy. The ground was littered with casualities; not only with dead men and dead horses but with horses and men not yet dead, able to crawl, to scream and to writhe. The lancers had perpetually to avoid riding over men they knew, men they had lived with and shared food and drink with, whilst riderless horses, some unhurt, some badly injured, tried to force their way into the ranks.[8]

The pall of smoke was so dense that they could see nothing in front of them. Suddenly they arrived at the low earthwork; their horses instinctively jumped and they were into the battery, into the sound of fighting and slaughter in the darkness. The smoke so obscured the sun that it was barely twilight, and in the gloom the British cavalry, maddened with excitement, cut and thrust and hacked like demons, while the Sikh gunners, with superb courage, fought to save or remove their guns. At last, they could do neither, the gunners left their seven heavy guns. They dashed back into the shelter of the squares formed by the regular Sikh infantry of Avitabile's brigade who were formed up in the rear of the battery, supported by a scattering of cavalry.[9]

Collecting themselves, the cavalry gathered speed to attack the squares that loomed, black and fringed with the flashes of musket-fire, out of the gloom; the bullets were flying around like a hailstorm. Right in the front of the regiment was Sergeant Harry Newsome, mounted on his grey charger. With a shout of

'Hullo, boys, here goes for death or a commission!' he forced his horse right over the front rank of kneeling men, on to their bayonets bristling above them like the quills on a porcupine's back. As Newsome dashed forward, he leant over and grasped one of the enemy's standards, but fell from his horse pierced by nineteen bayonet wounds. Into the gap made by Newsome they dashed but were given a terrible hammering by the resolute Sikh infantry.[10]

The sight of the lances seemed to paralyse the enemy, but they soon recovered and no quarter was given or asked. At first the British cavalry did spare some but found that these spared took up arms again and on some occasions actually killed the man who had just spared them; so the order was given to kill everyone bearing arms. The Sikh infantry had knelt at first to receive the charge and then rose, delivered their fire and boldly advanced with their swords and shields. Some lay on the ground so that the lances could not reach them while they either fired their muskets upwards at the men and horses or cut desperately at them with their keen swords. These Sikh infantrymen of the celebrated 'Aieen' troop of Avitabile fought most gallantly; they did not yield to the charge nor did they give way until they had been ridden over three times. So desperate was their defence that the lancers almost despaired of breaking them, until in a moment of inspiration they changed their lances over to their left hands, confusing the Sikhs and thus breaking them finally.

When the cavalry hit the squares at full gallop the shock was immense; lancers, men and horse, together with Sikh infantry, were overthrown in a shock stunning to both sides so that for a few seconds no man heeded another. Men were bruised and shaken; horses terrified and wedged in the crowd; bunches of figures sprawled in heaps and then struggled, dazed and stupid, to their feet, panting and looking wonderingly about them; several of the lancers even had time to remount. The Sikhs tried to hamstring the horses, they pressed their muskets into the very body of their opponent and fired them; they cut reins and stirrup-leathers, they slashed dexterously with their keen swords. They tried every device of cool, determined, disciplined men practised in war and trained to oppose cavalry.

The two forces seemed to be alone, in a private quarrel, the general battle forgotten. At one time 200 of the 16th Lancers were in the midst of over 5000 of the Sikh's choicest troops; there was no support for them and they were about three-quarters of a mile in advance of their line. After the battle many of the killed were found surrounded by dead Sikhs; Lance-Corporal Mowbray, the best lancer and swordsman in the regiment, was discovered with his lance splintered and his sword broken in a circle of seven dead Sikhs, the ground around him being ankle deep in blood. In another part of the field a 16th man was found sitting erect on his horse with his sword-arm raised in the act of striking. The horse was also erect in the act of crossing a nullah, with his legs extended – both were shot through the heart and must have died instantaneously. Major Smyth himself was very severely wounded in the waist by a bayonet thrust; he stuck to his horse manfully but was reeling in the saddle and was eventually taken to the rear by Sergeant Gould and a couple of men. The gallant Captain Bere took over until Captain Pearson came across, and a further charge was made into yet another square, which was broken. The conflict now developed into a series of small mêlées, with the Sikhs retiring on all sides.

Returning to find the regiment after taking Major Smyth back to the rear, Sergeant Gould and his party passed Sir Harry Smith. He looked approvingly at them and called out:

'Well done, the 16th! You have covered yourselves with glory!'

Sir Harry rode out to where the survivors of the 16th Lancers had re-formed; he noticed that 'C' Troop had no officers and asked where they were.

'All down, sir,' replied Sergeant Gould.

Sir Harry sadly shook his head:

'Then go and join the left wing under Major Bere.' Sir Harry rode over to Captain Pearson, who had assumed command of the regiment when Major Smyth was wounded, and congratulated him, saying:

'You may rely on me for a majority for this day's work'.

13

Battle Aftermath

The battle was by now nearly over; the fast-retreating Sikhs were being rapidly followed up by Wheeler's and Wilson's infantry brigades. The village of Bhundri was stormed and captured by H.M.'s 53rd Foot, who took many guns and cleared out the enemy infantry, who were not the disciplined regulars who faced the cavalry but the same irregular troops who fled from Aliwal village. As usual, the Sikh gunners resolutely stood their ground and fought to the death until the guns were finally taken at the bayonet point. Then two batteries of horse artillery came up to complete the discomfiture of the fleeing Sikh foot. A last gallant band of about 800 to 1000 strong, who had rallied under the shelter of a ravine, was dislodged by a flanking charge of the 30th Native Infantry and blasted out of existence by the fire of twelve guns at close range.

The entire Sikh force was now in utter rout and was being driven in complete confusion towards the ford by their camp; they were pursued by the cavalry, who made repeated charges and hemmed them in on their rear and both flanks by British infantry and artillery who tore them to pieces as they streamed away towards the river. Runjoor Singh had nine pieces unlimbered to cover the ford, but they only fired once before the pursuers were upon them. Unable to make any attempt to rally, the fugitives flung themselves in utter disorder into the river and such boats as they had, under a tempest of shot and shell from the British guns.

Runjoor attempted to bring away some of his guns, but had two spiked on the far bank of the river by Lieutenant Holmes of the Irregular Cavalry and Gunner Scott of the Horse Artillery, who forded the river in pursuit. No. 6 Company and the Light Company of the 50th Regiment were sent to the bank of the river to prevent a gun being taken away from the other side; the Sikhs tried several times to take it, crawling on their hands and knees, but a volley always drove them away. The men were partially undressed to go over by the ford to bring it over, but Sir Harry would not allow them to do so. They were eventually relieved by a company of sepoys who were left to prevent the gun being taken away, but in the morning it was gone. Runjoor also tried to form some sort of line on the opposite bank, but this was soon dissolved by a salvo from every piece of Smith's artillery. So the Sikh force streamed away in complete and utter defeat, with the loss of stores, camp, baggage, supplies and almost every one of their sixty-seven guns.

Said to have been almost unique in that it was 'a battle without a mistake in it', Aliwal signalled the end of Harry Smith's little campaign. He had brilliantly accomplished as awkward a task as had ever been set a general. With a small force Sir Harry had been sent to secure communication in one direction with Basseen (the route by which the siege train must arrive from Delhi) and in another with Ludhiana, and had to collect a handful of troops to help him engage a greatly superior enemy. In fact, Sir Harry had to career about the triangle formed by Dharmkot, Ludhiana and Basseen, each side of which was about twenty-five miles long, gathering together detachments of men in the presence of a concentrated enemy.

Characteristically, when he had all his men together he lost no time in marching to the attack; and the attack he made was no mere mad charge but a scientific application of the rules of war. Having struck the weak point at Aliwal village, Sir Harry concentrated eight of his eleven regiments of infantry on the enemy left. He left Wheeler's three battalions of infantry and McDowell's three cavalry regiments to deal with his centre and right. The result was that the losses of Wheeler and McDowell alone made up more than three-fourths of his casualty list, and the 16th Lancers formed more than one-fourth of it. Their charges of the two isolated squadrons first, then of the two remaining squadrons acting together, and finally of the whole regiment, were the most brilliant features of the whole action. Sir Harry Smith and Brigadier Cureton seemed to have timed them perfectly so that they shattered Runjoor Singh's last hopes of making a stand. It was a masterly stroke, but it cost the regiment the price of 144 officers and men, fifty-eight of them dead.[1] Some authorities have suggested that afterwards the ground was thickly strewn more with the bodies of the victorious horsemen than of the beaten infantry. Apart from the 16th Lancers, it is seldom that casualties are so evenly distributed among all units as those of Aliwal. The Duke of Wellington particularly admired the manner in which Sir Harry Smith utilised all three arms to the greatest possible advantage of each 'in this well-managed little affair'.

If the 16th Lancers had gone into action with parade-ground precision they returned in a very different condition, although in good spirits and exhilarated by their success. The infantry stood resting on their arms; their faces were black with powder after having bitten cartridges until there was a deep black circle around their mouths. The burnt powder from the ramrods had blackened their hands and in their efforts to remove the sweat from their faces they had completed the colouring from the roots of their hair to the chin. Concerned as they were with their own wounded and their share of the battle, they had their attention distracted by horses trotting, galloping or halting and gazing stupidly about them, terrified and bewildered. A dozen riderless troop horses went past them; others had men clinging helplessly to their saddles, lurching and covered with blood from perhaps a dozen deep gashes. Horses, streaming from tremendous gashes, limped and swayed with their riders, then followed the walking wounded in twos and threes. Men and horses were covered with blood and displaying terrible injuries – faces cut to rags, bowels protruding, fish-hook spears still stuck in their bodies. Men recognised their comrades; some running, some limping and some crawling, as the groups stumbled in; the infantry began to cheer them, men ran down to greet friends and wring them by the hand, as if they had struggled back from the depths of hell itself. Both men and horses of the remainder of the regiment were completely exhausted, many of the mounts being kept on their feet with difficulty.

The smoke settled, the roar of battle died away in a slow mumbling diminuendo, and the shadows began to deepen over the open grassland of the battle-field. On the gentle rise leading up to the small villages the thin groves of trees began to turn black against a sultry purple sunset.

The wounded, dying and dead of both sides covered the field in scores; they lay in shapeless masses, the usual mingling of the casualties of battle – scarlet-coated British infantrymen; blue-overalled cavalrymen; Khalsa soldiers and ragged hillmen; young officers and old sergeants, amid groups of horses and camels. The Sikh artillerymen were heaped around the captured guns that they had fought to the last; they revered their weapons and would only be parted from them by death.

In the hot sun the hundreds of dead horses had begun to swell and there was an awful growing odour of dead men and dead animals. The ground around the villages and inside the high earth-banked entrenchments was covered with men, horses, clothing, cartridge boxes, canteens, muskets, bayonets, scattered musket- and cannon-balls. Caissons and limbers stood where the horses had been killed by cannon-balls and had piled up on the pole just as they were killed.

In many places there was still a ghostly similarity to battle, as though the action had suddenly stopped short, leaving each man frozen in posture and attitude. Some kneeling behind small hummocks of rocks had met their death where they dropped for shelter. The muzzles of muskets resting upon rocks and stones had sightless, glassy eyes still gazing down their barrels and their guards gripped by hands convulsed in death. Numbers of Sikhs lay behind the earth wall they had erected; they had torn and twisted leaves of grass in their agonies and, faces buried in the loose soil, their mouths were filled with earth. Others lay in the ridiculous rag-doll postures of the dead, having crawled aside to some bush clump or ferny tuft, on receiving their death wound, to shelter; soaking grass, roots and soil with blood until, in lethargy, their eyes gazed in death. Some lay on their backs in the places where they had first dropped, their heels drumming incessantly on the soft ground until they had dug holes large enough to take a knapsack, before the involuntary movements slowed and finally ceased.

For the wounded, who covered the field so thickly, the bad part was just beginning. The anaesthesia of shock had worn off, the heat and sun had caused extreme discomfort, taking their minds off their bleeding, neglected wounds. Now the pain, thirst and chill of the Punjab winter's night was beginning to set in, causing them to moan and cry out. In the brave light of the sun, with their comrades on either side of them, whose comradeship coupled with discipline brought a stiffening resolution, then they had been men. Now in the fast-encroaching lonely dark they were reverting to little boys again. They cried for their mothers, for water, for help, for death, for God – the battle-field was eerily alive with a constant undercurrent of these low, pain-pitched voices, some shrilly Western and others gutturally Asiatic. The cold night air soon silenced many of the voices, wounded men died and stiffened quickly.

For the rest of the day and into the night the unwounded scoured the battle-field searching for the wounded. Although the battle noises had ended, there was no silence about the field. There was a moaning sound, rising and falling, multiplied a hundred times and intermingled with groans, curses, choking sobs, death-rattles and the swish of disabled men dragging themselves through the grass to a place of relief. Pistol-shots were crashing out as farriers went round despatching the wounded horses for which Mr Hurford, the 16th's Veterinary Surgeon, could do nothing. The men specially mourned the horses; one of the sergeant-majors was 'moved to tears when I thought of my beautiful horse; she was a light bay, nearly thoroughbred'.

The searchers passed through a litter of broken drums, abandoned muskets, shakoes, turbans, bitten cartridge-cases, split haversacks with their sparse rations trampled into a bloody slush, cast-off shoes and gaiters, treasured letters defiled with blood and dirt – an immense jumble-sale of Death. The streets of the two villages were a shambles, the horses, mules and camels, galloping about in terror, had trampled the bodies of the dead to mere masses of mangled flesh. The shells which had struck the houses had scattered grain, flour, ghee and every variety of article into the streets; in addition, everything had been thrown out of the houses by the soldiers of both sides, who hoped to find money under the floors or in the walls.

As the steps of the untrained litter-bearers slithered over the blood-soaked grass, they were chilled by the cries that rose on all sides from the heaving mass of mixed red and white, British and Sikh piled together.[2]

'Over here, for God's sake!'

'Water, water! I'm so thirsty!'

'Someone . . . please lift this dead man off my legs!'

'Damn you all! Can't anybody hear me? I need help . . . for God's sake!'

'Jist give me a 'and to me feet, sir . . . I think I can walk.'

'Don't mind me . . . go to that poor lancer chap . . . he's in awful pain.'

'Hallo, Rosie, I can't walk on the heath with you tonight . . . I seem to have hurt my leg.'

'Sections right! Jump to it! Come on, double up!'

'Hooray, the 53rd are first in the battery!'

'Sah, no keel me . . . I spik Inglish . . . no keel me.'

'Don't think I'm hurt bad, sir . . . did we win?'

'We licked 'em? Hooray!'

'Tell 'Arry Smith that Private Simms of the 53rd 'opes 'e's made a dook for this day's work!'

14

Back in Camp

Back in Sir Hugh Gough's main camp the fortunes of Sir Harry Smith's force were causing considerable anxiety. The mission on which they had been sent was of paramount importance and with the news of the humiliating loss of baggage during the Badowal march it seemed as though success was going to elude Sir Harry.

On the morning of the 28th, the day of the Battle of Aliwal, the sound of artillery could be heard in the camp and an officer who was with Sir Hugh wrote of the scene:

'From not having heard of Sir Harry Smith and various native rumours about the camp, Sir Hugh was really very miserably anxious about him and the fine force he had given him; and I must now tell you of that gallant, glorious, good old chief. We heard the cannonading which was, while it lasted, fearful. I asked him what he thought of it.

' "Think of it! Why, 'tis the most glorious thing I ever heard. Sure, I can tell by the sound of the guns that Smith has carried the position and silenced their artillery."

' "I hope so, sir," I said, "he has not found it too strong, and retired to wait for our reinforcements."

' "Retire!" he cried. "No! Never! No British force would ever retire before such a cannonade as we have just heard!"

'He spoke with such likely confidence that, although I had gone to him fully impressed with the conviction that Smith had failed, I left him perfectly assured that I was wrong, and that victory had been ours. He sent Bagot and Beecher to bring an express. When he heard the news he was nearly frantic with joy! But Bagot told me that ere the lapse of two minutes he saw the dear old man on his knees by his couch, offering up his thanks to the Power which alone gave us the victory.'

A trooper of the 16th Lancers, named Eaton, who was apparently with the party that brought the news of the victory to Sir Hugh, writing on the 2nd February 1846, says:

'As soon as the Commander-in-Chief received the despatches, which he did on horseback while reconnoitring, he leapt from his horse and gave three cheers, a salute of eighteen guns was fired, and the line gave three hearty cheers for us, their gallant comrades, as they called us.'

The Governor-General issued a general order announcing the victory, congratulating the commander and his force, and extolling their valour, discipline and skill in well-deserved terms. A gala parade of the whole force of the main army was ordered, and as the two chiefs rode down the line to announce the victory, they were greeted by cheers such as an Englishman alone can give. By order of the Governor-General a royal salute was fired from the British camp, the regimental bands playing the National Anthem. The Sikhs, on the opposite bank of the River Sutlej, not to be outdone, followed suit with both, and their bands were heard lustily playing 'God Save the Queen'!

When Sir Harry Smith and his victorious force arrived back in the main camp of February 8th, 1846, they were enthusiastically received by all ranks, who were probably not slow to notice that the lancers had lost nearly a third of their number. Sir Hugh Gough addressed each corps in terms as gratifying to them as they were to Sir Harry Smith, and then proceeded to dine Sir Harry, his staff, commanding officers of corps and Prince Waldemar of Prussia (travelling as Count Ravensburg, who was present with his suite at the battles of Mudki, Ferozeshah, Aliwal and Sobraon), during which he drank their good healths and praised them highly in his speech. To the Commander-in-Chief the victory came at a most opportune moment; he had gained costly success at Mudki and Ferozeshah, the latter not very far removed from failure, and his sepoys shrank more and more from again meeting the Sikhs. Now the dreaded enemy had not only been defeated but had been harried, hunted and humiliated. His utter inability to make more than an honourable stand against the British forces on a fair field, even with a marked superiority in numbers and in guns, had been more than proved.

Owing to Sir Harry Smith's force being detached from the main army and the rapid movements that had been made at only a few hours' notice, the arrangements for the field hospital were by no means complete and the unfortunate wounded suffered greatly, being without proper food or shelter. The operating theatres and the wards themselves, one and the same place on most occasions, were merely tents, stifling in daytime and bitterly cold at night. The wounded lay on the ground in the blankets saturated with blood and ordure in which they had been brought from the battle-field. There were no cots or mattresses, the only available 'hospital comforts' being rice-water and coarse wheaten-cake as prepared for the elephants. Some of them lay without a drink of water all that night and through the next day, there were no cups or buckets to bring water in. The regimental surgeons did their best, but there were serious deficiences, wastes and want of system in the governmental supply of nursing stores, medicines and the other necessary items for the care of the wounded. As was to be tragically revealed nine years later in the Crimea, there were plenty of the right sort of stores but they were never where they were needed; the complicated, frustrating supply system made harrowing experiences of the days following a battle. Hundreds of wounded men, not necessarily noble or brave, but soldiers who had been grievously hurt doing their duty, were allowed to lie helpless, mangled, faint and alone; to bleed to death or to die from sheer exhaustion and exposure; often actually untouched by doctors or merely laid down and left through sheer lack of trained personnel and equipment with which to save them.[1]

After Aliwal those who could be moved were transported to the large hospital at Ferozepor, which housed the many wounded of Mudki and Ferozeshah. This place was probably no better or no worse than any other military hospital of the period; it was totally lacking in equipment, there was no furniture and few medical supplies; in fact hardly enough of the ordinary necessities of life. The regulations of the British Army laid down that each soldier should bring his pack into hospital with him, and his pack contained a change of clothing and eating utensils. But most of the soldiers had abandoned their packs in order to keep up on the ardous marches under the hot sun and in the sandy, dusty earth. According to the same regulations, a private soldier in hospital was placed on what was known as a whole diet, a half-diet or a spoon diet. The first was the man's ordinary rations cooked for him by the hospital, the second about half his rations, and the third was liquid food. In addition, he was supposed to receive extra diet in the form of milk, butter, eggs, arrowroot, jellies, etc. But the cooking facilities were meagre; the tea made in the same kettles in which the meat had just been boiled, and, as water was short, the kettles were not cleaned and the tea was undrinkable. The meat for the ward was issued to the orderly, who tied it up, put some distinguishing mark on it – such as a piece of dirty rag, a button, old nail or bit of torn uniform – and then dropped into the communal pot. The water did not really boil; when he considered enough time had elapsed, the orderly fished in the pot with a piece of wood or a ramrod for his own portion, often knocking it all over and extinguishing the fire, so that the portions put in last of all were eaten almost raw. The meat was divided up on the orderly's bed, and eaten with the fingers; it was cold and congealed because of the time that had elapsed since it was taken from the pot. Men on the spoon diet got the water in which the meat had been cooked.

Huge wooden tubs stood in the wards for the men to use as latrines; the orderlies disliked the unpleasant job of emptying them and they were left for twenty-four hours on end, to slop over and stink in the close atmosphere of the shuttered buildings and the baking tents. Whatever the patient had when he entered, he soon acquired the prevailing condition of diarrhoea. This produced a condition of sheer physical weakness that reduced his chances of recovering from the shattering effects of his wound and subsequent surgical treatment. In military hospitals of the day, and later in the Crimea, the majority of men who lived long enough after their initial surgery to be admitted, died not of their wounds but of disease they contracted as a result of being in the hospital. It is remarkable that anyone survived at all; it says much for the hardness and innate toughness of the British soldier that he emerged from such ordeals and lived to fight another day.

Under such conditions, Captain W. B. Thomson and Lieutenant Goodwyn did their best to aid the wounded, who were visited frequently by the Governor-General, Sir Henry Hardinge, who '. . . delighted the men by his urbanity and kindness so that they forgot their sufferings in the admiration which his kindness elicited . . .' It is recorded that if a man had lost an arm the Governor-General would point to his own empty sleeve and assure them that it would soon be all right; if a soldier had a leg shot away or shattered he reminded him that one of his own sons, who was with him, had gone into battle at his side with only one foot.

Taking into consideration all the known facts concerning treatment of wounded soldiers during this period of military history, it is not clear who were luckiest – the sixty officers and men of the 16th Lancers who lost their lives at Badowal and Aliwal or the seventy-seven all ranks who were only wounded!

Notes

Chapter 1. *Note* 1

In 1842, at the time when the events related in this book began, Ireland presented the extraordinary spectacle of a country in which employment and wages scarcely existed. There were no industries and very few farms large enough to need to employ labour. The people lived in mud huts, four or five feet high; they were built on the bare earth, roofed with boughs and turf sods; they had no chimneys or windows. Without any sort of furniture, amid almost indescribable squalor, human beings and animals slept together on the earth floor.

Lacking land and implements, the Irish peasants tried to alleviate their desperate poverty by adopting the potato as their staple food. Potatoes require only one-third of the acreage required for wheat, they will flourish literally anywhere; they need little cultivation and can be stored in the ground, besides all this they could be shared with the pigs and the fowls. By using a 'lazy bed' that required only the use of a spade to cover them with earth, the Irish grew 'horse potatoes' – the largest, coarsest and most prolific variety known. They ate this potato boiled and they ate nothing else; other vegetables and bread were unknown, there were no butchers, bakers or grocers.

The population spread like a prairie fire because religion and ignorance made birth-control unthinkable; girls were usually married before they were sixteen and were grandmothers in their early thirties. Swarming in the fields and cabins, the rapidly increasing numbers had no employment nor any way of obtaining wages; if the potato crop failed there was no means of escaping starvation.

In the 1840s this disaster occurred; dire distress followed and famine began in earnest until the country spawned starving multitudes plaintively crying for food. Dead bodies lay by the sides of the roads; in remote hamlets every soul perished, having become too weak to fly from death. It was not long before everyone had the word 'emigrate' on their lips; to get to Canada or Australia, but, above all, the United States of America, seemed to spell safety. So the roads to the ports of Ireland became thronged with weakly moving people trying to escape almost certain death. Lack of money prevented many of them from leaving the land of their birth, but for as little as half a crown they could be transported across the Irish Channel. Like an avalanche, the starving and destitute Irish flooded into the industrial towns of England; it was not possible to find work for them all and many of them found that they had exchanged the position of starving in the midst of nothing to that of hunger in the midst of plenty.

The young men found in the British Army a means of obtaining food and clothing, to say nothing of a roof over their heads; regimental rolls began to resemble Irish parish registers and the march of the British Empire in India was milestoned by graves bearing Irish names.

Chapter 1. *Note* 2

Criminals were often spared punishment by county J.P.s and sometimes even released from prison or sentence of transportation to serve in the Army; thus the Army became an asylum for the scourings of the nation. Because of bad treatment, small pay and appalling housing it was difficult to obtain recruits and they had to be inveigled into the Army by questionable methods. If there was no counterpart to the naval press-gangs, many recruits were obtained by means hardly less deplorable. But for many years it was still 'Jack Frost' who was the best recruiting sergeant; it was still stark necessity which drove many men to enlist. At current rates of pay. still low even for the period, the recruits would necessarily be drawn from the lower ranks of labour; unemployment benefit did not exist in those days.

In some cases the recruit was attracted to the service by a sum of money called bounty, which varied in amount. This meant that many of the recruits were respectable, docile country lads; countrymen were always preferred by the officers and the lad who had been brought up by careful, thrifty parents in a decent cottage home was most heartily welcomed to the Colours.

The recruiter received fifteen shillings 'bringing money' for every man that he produced; this meant that he did not bother himself about anything more than the recruit's physical fitness. In this manner a great many men enlisted were of the criminal class or were mentally deficient; from the days of the Restoration these dregs of the nation had formed a large proportion of the men in the ranks, so that the Army in the 1840s consisted largely of hardened soldiers of the old school, many of them were prematurely aged through the hard barrack life and others were undermined by drink. The majority were illiterate; but they were stolid, shrewd and long-suffering; their language was coarse and blasphemous and they suffered from a thirst that needed eternally slaking.

Such men corrupted the self-respecting elements in the barrack-room; the influences to which the recruit was subjected at the outset were not calculated to uplift him. Soon he nurtured a hatred for the military system that clothed and fed him; this was a situation fostered by the fact that the unfortunate recruit did not receive one penny of wages until he had served for some months, owing to the instalments taken from his pay to cover the constant debt into which the system brought him.

The billets in which the men lived were often sinks of iniquity or squalor; it was not long since they were housed in the lowest ale-houses in the country. Even the King's Guards were stowed away in the Royal Mews or in buildings that were notoriously insanitary even for the period. The soldier had little to look forward to – on some of the West India stations his life expectancy was only a couple of years, and yellow fever and cholera abounded on all the tropical stations. If he survived he was eventually discharged with impaired health and a pension of a few pence a day; being a beggar was the normal trade of the veteran.

By painting an inaccurate picture of the advantage of a military career, unscrupulous recruiting sergeants cajoled many unsophisticated men into the Army. The airy promise of a smart uniform, a horse to ride and a sword to wield, plus unlimited money to spend, exercised a hypnotic effect upon such a youth. The recruiter would 'blow the trumpet and bang the drum in lusty fashion'.

'Best bit of work I ever did was to take the Queen's Shilling! Soldiering is a fine life – lots of money, lots of beer and lots of girls! No anxieties . . . you get rations, lodgings, clothing and education. If you die, a first-class funeral with a band and a firing-party. You get a chance of seeing the world too . . . why, every soldier can have two servants of his own in India . . . they clean your kit and you can kick 'em like dogs if they don't do it proper! What's more, a chance of rising Lootenant after a year or two easy work . . . and maybe Colonel before you finish your time. I've had two comrades become regimental commanders in my day and should have done so myself . . . but I never had your education when I was a boy, which sort of kept me back. It's better than being a civilian! Now, lad, except for this one vacancy our regimental strength is full! Make up your mind now. . . it's yes or no!'

When he had accepted the bright new shilling from the Recruiting Sergeant the military confidence trick had once again been successful. To prove it, a ribbon from the knot of the Sergeant's cap was pinned on to the recruit to show that he had taken the Queen's Shilling. From then on he was not let out of the Sergeant's sight until handed over to the escorting non-commissioned officer.

Chapter 1. *Note* 3

In the early 1840s the young Queen Victoria had yet to complete the first ten years of her lengthy reign and Stephenson's *Rocket* had only recently chuffed its pioneer run from Darlington to Stockton. The British Army was nearly 200 years old; for the entire period of its existence it had been treated with contempt, dislike and neglect by the nation it served – even in a period when it was saving its existence, protecting its trade or building its Empire.

When it is considered that the eighteenth and early nineteenth centuries were epochs of habitual brutality and hard living, when wages were at starvation level and barbarous punishments commonplace, it is not really remarkable that the soldier should have been dogged with the reputation of violence and evil-living. Even so, it cannot be denied that the life of the soldier of the day stood out as one which offered hardly any compensation for its discomforts and hazards. The soldier's vices were probably no worse nor more frequent than those of the civilian of the period. This consideration appears to have escaped notice when heaping abuse on military heads, nor was any notice taken of the extenuating circumstances provided by his miserable service-life conditions.

When a man joined up he was in for a pretty rough time, not only from his fellows and his superiors in the Army itself but also from the whole population outside. Influential in moulding the derisive tone habitually used when talking of the soldier during the period immediately before the Crimean War, writer Michael Titmarsh said in *Punch*:

'The whole system of the Army is something egregious and artificial. The civilian who lives out of it cannot understand it. It is not like other professions which require intelligence. A man one degree removed from idiocy, with brains sufficient to direct his powers of mischief and endurance, may make a distinguished soldier. As to the men, they get the word of command to advance or to fall back, and they do it; they are told to strip and be flogged, and they do it; or to flog, and they do it; to murder or be murdered, and they obey; for their food and clothing and twopence a day for their tobacco.'

For an employee to 'go for a soldier' was even considered to reflect upon his erstwhile employers; a contemporary conversation taken from a novel* about the period is enlightening. The dignified ex-employer is expostulating with the Recruiting Sergeant:

' "... think of the disgrace to Hepplewhite Brothers! What will they think of me in the Lane? What will they say to me at the next Mansion House banquet? I've had boys that ran off to sea, and boys that embezzled the petty cash, and boys that were locked up for assaulting police officers. But a boy who did this thing I've

**Trumpeter Sound*, by D. L. Murray (Hodder and Stoughton), London 1933.

never had in the warehouse before!"

' "Beggin' your pardon, sir, but I don't see nothing disgraceful in serving the Queen against her enemies. Moreover, it's a fine roving life for a young fellow."

' "Is it indeed? I beg to differ from you, my friend. I'd rather see this boy in a convict transport than in the Army! Why? Because a convict can't do any more harm and a soldier can! That's why!" '

In spite of this background of prejudice the Army established the finest of traditions and a most illustrious history. At the time in question it was about to begin the series of 'small colonial wars' that brought Queen Victoria her vast overseas Empire. The dregs of the nation impressed into the semblance of an army have only needed appropriate training, discipline and command to be converted in a relatively short space of time from an armed rabble into an effective instrument of war. Dr Johnson, who saw shrewdly into most things, once wrote some thoughts on the British soldier. He began thus:

'The qualities which commonly make an army formidable are long habits of regularity, great exactness of discipline and great confidence in the commander.'

He went on to show that regularity is no part of the English soldier's character, that their discipline was often indifferent and that they had no particular reason to be confident in their commander; yet they were without doubt the bravest soldiers in Europe. He ascribed it to the independence of character of the Englishmen who calls no man his master. He ended his essay thus:

'Those who complain in peace of the insolence of the populace must remember that their insolence in peace is bravery in war.'

Let the last word fittingly rest with a Victorian novelist, Ouida, who wrote:

'There ain't better stuff to make soldiers with than Englishmen; but they're badgered – 'orrible badgered!'

Chapter 1. *Note* 4

The Barrack Department apparently specialised in erecting gaunt, grim barrack buildings that had a special brand of stark rectangular ugliness. The setting for this particular military camp at Hounslow had quite possibly been influenced by its suitability for the manoeuvres of horses and guns over the wide stretching sandy wastes. It was also part of the policy of the Duke of Wellington (whose slightest word was law where military matters were concerned); he dreaded that the House of Commons should dangerously reduce the forces so he withdrew the Army as much as possible from public observation. This still further dissociated the country from its armed defenders.

Chapter 1. *Note* 5
If it is to be accepted that the soldier deserved popular derision then it was derision arising from his besetting sin of habitual drunkenness. The oblivion of cheap alcohol did much to blot out for a few hours the misery and squalor of his life.

The men might drink, blaspheme, cheat the recruit – all customs hallowed by time – but active service had always proved their mettle, the traditional regimental spirit was there, and that sufficed. So why change? Such arguments and attitudes took no account of the dreadful conditions under which the soldier lived, the crowding in the barrack-rooms, the faulty food and foul hygiene. How many men had deserted in disgust at these sordid conditions, how many had succumbed to a moment's rage or a spasmodic revolt against a crushing disciplinary system?

Chapter 1. *Note* 6
A wide chasm separated the officer from the soldier in peace-time, the officers only appearing on parade when their presence might be required for the performance of some drill or parade by the whole regiment – at other times daily barrack-square routine could be managed by the Sergeant-Major and his underlings, with the Adjutant or an orderly officer in the background or supervising the exercises from a chair in a convenient window. This worked reasonably well because many officers had only the vaguest ideas as to what was going on, having purchased their commissions and possessing only a modicum of military training.

The life of the officer being what it was, it is no surprise that his intellectual level should leave much to be desired – he had an antipathy towards all theory, to everything abstract; an innate contempt for things savouring of mere learning or bookwork, contempt for any intellectual superiority was as harmful as it was widespread. The Duke of Wellington, bursting out in despair, said:

'We have seen many changes, but they have all come at the right time and the right time for change is when you can't help it!'

The attitude of the young cavalry officer is, perhaps a little harshly, reflected by the remark made by one of them:

'. . . the Army is all right so long as it is limited to the Mess and the band, but the troops are a damned nuisance!'

The generals and officers were the counterparts of the regiments they commanded. Just as the rank and file were typical of the British nation at large, so the higher ranks were representative of the landed gentry whence the majority of them at that time were drawn. They had the same standards of duty, the same rigid code of morals, being slaves to appearance and to an accepted code of manners that rested mainly on external details. But in the Army these qualities were supported by the more rigid code that had governed military life since the days of the Peninsular, and that had been hallowed by the passing of the years. The officer class of Victorian days remained as close a trade union as ever existed. Even when the gentry were reinforced from the world of industry and commerce the newcomers were soon inoculated with the ideas and the standards they saw about them until they were swallowed by their surroundings.

In England, thirty years after Waterloo, men had forgotten the harsh lessons of the Napoleonic campaigns, of the miseries of the retreat from Corunna, of the rags and fevers, the fears and agonies of Walcheren; they still dreamed of military glory, forgot that valour and gallantry are invariably sacrificed to stupidity and corruption and that splendid armies are often defeated by starvation, pestilence and filth. Since Time began, men's imaginations have been seized and their minds set on fire by the thought of the excitement of combat, the glory of victory, by the trumpets, the plumes and the colours. Intoxicatedly, men turn eagerly to war, dreaming of commanding large armies and performing deeds of valour that will make them famous – indeed did not the Duke himself personify all that filled their minds? But this was no dream for the comman man, for the ordinary soldier! Obviously, war was an aristocratic trade that should be reserved for princes and nobles trained and educated to be brave so that they knew battles to be won only by bravery, courage and valour – courage was esteemed to be the one essential military quality and it was a virtue exclusive to the aristocrat. The very nature of the Army's training during this period excited the blood and encouraged such thoughts – the lust for power and glory being nourished by the long, obedient lines of colourful infantry forming and re-forming on the parade ground and the gilt-encrusted glittering squadrons of cavalry, prancing and wheeling in obedience to the strings pulled by their commanding officers. Among these officers there existed an heirloom of the eighteenth-century gentlemen of England, an appreciation of good horsemanship.

Chapter 2. *Note* 1

After Waterloo came a period of reaction; the great victory was followed by a strong – perhaps natural – revulsion towards the military activities of the past twenty years. The nation was, in fact, heartily sick of wars and soldiers. The politicians knew that the Army could not be destroyed, so they decided that it should be banished. Their methods of doing this largely revolved around their becoming ever increasingly parsimonious in sanctioning any expenditure on the fighting services. For example, the principle that governed design in the housing of the other ranks of the period was that as little money as possible must be spent upon the building and as many men as possible crammed into it. It is difficult to understand the reasoning of legislators who provided

1000 cubic feet of space for each convict but thought 300 feet enough for a soldier.

Whilst the economists on the one hand complained about the cost of recruits, on the other hand they laid themselves out to kill them off as rapidly as possible through the conditions under which they made them exist. However, the Napoleonic Wars and the small colonial wars of the period, coupled with public maltreatment, had drawn officers and men closer together than in the past. In some regiments officers were giving considerable thought to bettering the lot of their men and in so doing went a way towards combating the meanness of the State. There was little they could do about the actual construction of the insanitary barracks but they tried to make the men keep them as clean as possible.

During the long years of peace that followed Waterloo in 1815 the British soldier found very little improvement in conditions of service, pay, housing, equipment and training. But public conscience was beginning to stir, at first over issues like slavery and the improvement of prisons and then about the fighting services. The former brought new legislation but the War Office entrenched itself behind walls of tradition and archaic discipline when such challenges arose. They pleaded that such changes would be dangerous and would undermine the military order that had brought such glorious victories in the past. At the same time they could and did seriously let every military department run down so that the stores of war sank well below the danger level. Thus was produced the wild wind that was to be painfully reaped in the Crimea.

In reality, however honest or realistic the military administration might wish to be, they had got themselves so hopelessly involved in red tape and detailed regulations that even the most minor changes were hardly possible without years of argument and discussion.

Chapter 2. *Note* 2

The first barrack regulations ever printed sanctioned the married soldier to annex a corner of the barrack-room as his family's home. The regulation commended the practice 'for the greater cleanliness and convenience of the soldier . . .' The provision was no more than a logical continuation of the practice of women being permitted to follow the troops in the capacity of cooks and sutlers – customary during Marlborough's wars and earlier.

Six women per troop were the numbers officially allowed in barracks; this was the same number as were allowed to follow their husbands overseas on active service. In return for this sparse accommodation the soldier's wife cooked for the room, washed for its occupants and performed various household tasks, services for which she was allowed a meagre pittance stopped from the men's pay.

Barrack-room life was a hard existence for a woman; it was one that did not permit many outward displays of obviously womanly feelings. The authorities maintained that the existence of the 'married corner' benefited the morals of the barrack-room because it tended to check the profanity that marked the period. What it did for those who lived their young lives crowded behind this flimsy screen is not hard to imagine. The children were treated almost as pets by the other soldiers in the barrack-room; taught to gulp down large draughts of ale, pull at foul pipes and repeat strange oaths. Even a grown-up daughter would have to crowd in behind the blanket to sleep wherever she could find space: boys, lucky by reason of their sex, were able to utilise the beds left vacant by soldiers on guard or in hospital.

Most of the efforts at improving the lot of the married soldier in the mid-nineteenth century came to an abrupt halt when requests were invariably answered by the usual excuse: 'No funds available'.

Chapter 2. *Note* 3

Breakfast messes made their appearance in the 1820s; before that time it had been customary for each man to make his own provision for breakfast. This meant that some men had nothing, others bread and water or what their fancy and means permitted. It was a common practice for the soldiers' wives and widows to eke out a scanty living by selling bread and coffee or tea to the troops in the early morning. In this way men on guard or on detachment who would possibly otherwise miss their breakfast could provide for themselves on the spot. When breakfast messes came into use this custom died out.

Meals were eaten in the barrack-room; boards and trestles were dragged out into the narrow alley between the lines of cots and the men would perch on the foot of their beds, as there were no chairs.

Chapter 2. *Note* 4

In some ways armies have always seemed to be almost childlike in the earnest pride they feel over regimental facings and subtle customs. But these things were the stuff that made the regimental feeling that inspired and encouraged the soldiers of Queen Victoria's army. The small colonial wars of the period were viewed as colourful affairs by both officers and men. They were fought in exactly the same uniforms that were worn on church parades in peaceful English garrison towns. It was as though a labourer had decided in a momentary spirit of gay abandon to go to work in his best suit; so the Army went to war in scarlet and gold. In a few weeks their gold lace was in shreds, their bright tunics in ribbons, but they would remain splendid in their rags as they set about learning how to beat the Zulus on the veldt or the Afghan tribesmen in their rocky hills.

It was a picturesque army; it wore scarlet jackets, white helmets or havelocks; blue trousers with broad red stripe down the side. Or, in moments of unparalleled freedom, the men were issued with white duck trousers! Thus tradition was upheld, ritual and ceremony were preserved as far as possible and spirits remained high.

Chapter 2. *Note* 5

The way in which food was served out in the barrack-room caused considerable dissatisfaction among the men. It was the custom for each member of the mess to turn round so that he could not see what the carver had in front of him. The carver would then tap with his knife on each plate, calling out: 'Who shall have this?'

It was possible by intonation and custom for the carver to indicate the intended destination of any particular portion – when the word 'shall' was strongly emphasised it was meant to go to a recruit or new soldier who would find himself faced with a plateful of fat, bone and gristle. Thus, the name given to the ration when it was cup up was 'the who shall', and it was 'bobbed-out'.

Chapter 2. *Note* 6

The daily ration was one pound of bread and three-quarters of a pound of meat. The only cooking utensils or appliances provided by the authorities were two coppers per squadron – one for the meat and the other for the potatoes. The men took it in turns to cook; they needed little culinary knowledge to do this – all that was required of them was to boil the meat. There was no variety because there were no means of roasting or baking the meat; every man received each day a solid portion of boiled beef served up in a liquid portion of broth, with boiled potatoes and bread.

The soldier had but two meals a day, then came a nineteen-hour interval without any food whatsoever. Even so, the savage hunger brought on by the strenuous physical work often failed to make the nauseating diet more palatable. In the course of time the soldier would lose his interest in food and would consume tastelessly whatever was slapped down in front of him. He no longer felt resentment when his share turned out to be all bone or all gristle – someone had to have this portion in the rigid weighing out of rations.

Chapter 2. *Note* 7

In our military history there are few more familiar incidents than the stubborn resistance of the British line at Waterloo. Silent and immovable through the long hours of the midsummer day the squares and squadrons stood in the trampled corn, forbidden to reply to the fire of cannon and of musketry that harassed them incessantly. The bullets of the skirmishers whistled round them and the great roundshot tore through the tight-packed ranks. Men fell headlong in the furrows, some without even a cry of pain. Throughout this nightmare the word was quietly passed round the squares:

'Close in on the centre, men!'

The formations stood fast upon the ground they had held since noon; depleted in number and shoulder to shoulder as the sun began to set.

It is rare indeed in military history that a British regiment has not held together. One great truth stands out – whenever the British soldier has taken the field properly trained and fed, adequately armed and supplied, he has invarably responded wholeheartedly to any calls made upon him by his country and his commanders. On many occasions by a typical display of his own stubborn courage he has redeemed grave errors of leadership. Defects and oversights in military management and miscalculations in the conduct of a campaign have nearly always been at the bottom of his few failures.

Chapter 3. *Note* 1

It was the opinion of the authorities that nothing much mattered provided the fighting qualities of the men survived, together with ancient traditions they made success certain. Things went on in a happy-go-lucky sort of fashion so far as actual military training was concerned. Ceremonial parades and similar exercises being the principal activity, no training except for the relatively meaningless barrack-square drill was given. This atmosphere of make-believe meant that foreign officers were prone to write:

'. . . In England I never saw or heard of cavalry being taught to charge, disperse and form . . . to give officers and men any idea of outpost duty was considered absurd and it all had to be learned when they came abroad.'

Often learned at the cost of life and limb.

The fact was that there was no one who could teach them – because no one knew anything about it. The experiences gained during the Napoleonic Wars, now thirty years behind them, had long since been forgotten.

Chapter 3. *Note* 2

The swords in use had been first issued in 1823; they were to continue in much the same form until 1908 when the straight thrusting sword was supplied. The blade was thirty-six inches in length, with a thick, heavy back; the hilt-guard had three bars with considerable spaces between them; the grip was of horn, thick and almost round, so that a firm grip with a gloved hand was almost impossible; the blade was slightly curved. The sword may be said to have combined in itself every possible fault that a sword could have. It was at once too short, too heavy, too blunt and apt to turn in the hand so that in the excitement of an action the cut as often as not was made with the flat.

Chapter 3. *Note* 3
There were no special amenities and few, of any, facilities for the soldiers' recreation.

Education in the Army was almost non-existent, fear of revolutionary propaganda preventing any educational reform taking place.

'By jove!' exclaimed the old Duke of Wellington, 'if ever there is a mutiny in the Army – and in all probability we shall have one – you'll see that these new-fangled schoolmasters will be at the bottom of it!'

In 1846 Sidney Herbert, then Secretary at War, introduced a new system of education in the Army, but nothing was really accomplished until after the Crimean upheaval. At that time the percentage of illiterates in the infantry was 60 per cent, and no desire could be ascertained among the soldier for any improvement in this matter! Of course, the soldier soon learned the 'tricks of the trade' – some useful, such as the proper care of his feet on the march, of his weapons and equipment at all times, the secret of making the best of uncomfortable conditions – some bad, such as scrounging or looting.

Owing to the desire to prevent subversive literature being read by the soldiers, only a prescribed list of some twenty-eight books, all approved by a bench of bishops, were permitted into barracks.

Chapter 3. *Note* 4
The Duke of Wellington had always opposed any increase in the soldiers' pay for the reason that if the Army became more costly the nation would resent such increased charges. In the Commons a number of Members of Parliament voted against any such proposals because they claimed that more pay would only make the Army more licentious and that such a situation would only end in greater severity of discipline to act as a deterrent. Nevertheless, some slight variations were introduced and it was decided that the soldier's pay should be graduated according to his length of service and that good-conduct pay should be instituted. In 1800 one penny extra per day was granted as 'beer money', in 1806 another penny per day, awarded to every soldier who had completed seven years' service and twopence per day to those with fourteen years. In 1845 a penny per day good-conduct was awarded for every seven years' complete service. In 1847 it was decreed that no soldier should ever receive less than one penny per day actual cash.

Finally in 1854 the daily stoppage made for a man's rations was reduced from sixpence to fourpence-halfpenny. Thus at the outbreak of the Crimean War the soldier received a minimum of one shilling per day and one penny per day beer money; from this total was deducted fourpence-halfpenny for cost of rations, and from the remaining eightpence-halfpenny per day was subtracted the regimental stoppages and cost of his necessaries. But, like every other good military intention, much of this foundered on the rock formed by the Pay Sergeant. This individual had over the years developed various tricks for keeping back men's pay on the pretext that they must hold a certain deposit to cover the necessary outlay for replacing clothing and necessaries. The practice sometimes meant that as much as six months' pay was held back. This was a practice much resented by the men, who objected to having their pay stopped in order to allow a Pay Sergeant to pay for clothing for men already in debt and to enable him to profit from a creditor's sudden death.

Chapter 3. *Note* 5

Perhaps because the ale was consumed more to produce a stupor that blotted out the misery and squalor of their monotonous, bullied lives than for amusement or sociability, few men got genially drunk.

Drunk in sufficient quantities, the cheap ale would give a man a temporary belief that he was more than an unthinking animal who blindly obeyed all orders hurled at him. Inversely, it could make him hypersensitive to fancied slights and insults from men of his own level, resulting in the brawls that rid his body of the pent-up venom and frustration brought on by his daily life. Except by snatches of deep, exhausted sleep in the stinking, stuffy barrack-room, there was no other way but drink for a man to forget that he had placed himself in an intolerable situation. A situation where every waking moment was at the whim of someone in a superior position who could sadistically make his life a misery or, at best, keep him on his toes in a world of barked commands, implicit discipline and harsh punishments for offences and omissions.

Chapter 3. *Note* 6

It has been written in contemporary accounts that the streets of garrison towns were nightly full of drunken, reeling men in black and ugly moods, spoiling for trouble. Dangerous antipathies existed between regiments, arising out of some obscure or fancied slight that had occurred years before on active service – such and such a unit had not done their share on the rearguard during Moore's retreat to Corunna thirty-odd years before or the 43rd Foot had not seen as much action at Waterloo as had the 92nd. These real or imaginary grievances survived in the form of ancient feuds that shook garrison towns to their very foundations on pay nights when grim purposeful mauls were fought out with bare fists, belts, bottles, sticks, stones and sometimes bayonets.

It was pay day that usually saw these fracas because only then did the soldier have money to buy enough drink to get quarrelsome. To ensure that neighbouring units did not get drunk on the same night, a system of 'staggered' pay days came into being so that the various units did not receive their pay on the same day.

Once the brawling had started the men were allowed to fight it out for a while so as to 'work off steam'; then the hysterical trumpets would screech out in the nearby barracks and patrols would double out bearing pickaxe handles. Being sober and having had their rest disturbed, these squads would not be too fussy about the way they used their weapons; so the men they dragged tottering back to barracks, sometimes in handcuffs, would often be considerably roughed-up.

Chapter 3. *Note* 7

It was not considered particularly important in the cavalry for a man to be able to fire competently a carbine or pistol. They were élite light troops whose principal function was to swoop in closely at the enemy and demoralise or demolish him with long lance or heavy sword, swooping gracefully out when the job was done. This did not always work out successfully, as infantry appeared to be ignorant of the rules of the game, usually forming a tight formation and emptying saddles with musket-fire long before they got close enough to use cold steel.

Chapter 3. *Note* 8

Throughout the ages cavalrymen have been a class of their own, treating warfare as a glorified 'hunt' (less the hounds) and claiming all nature of exaggerated success at the high cost of the soft flesh of men and horses. The hallmarks of a good officer in the heyday of the Victorian army were the possession of a good horse and the ability to ride it well. A fine string of hunters, the capacity for an occasional hunt in the 'Shires', a smart turn-out in a garrison town – all these things went a very long way towards forming a real claim to military advancement.

Perhaps it is too easy to scoff; it cannot be denied that such high standards of individual gallantry and daring horsemanship proved of the utmost value during the Army's 'Small Wars' and particularly showed to advantage in the Indian Mutiny, for example.

Chapter 3. *Note* 9

The men in the ranks, who usually averaged about twelve years' service, went through the movements of pivot-drill like machines. They were accustomed to taking the bit between their teeth and obeying the Commanding Officer's word of command without regard for the mistakes of their troop leaders. So complicated was this system that it was impossible, for example, to reverse the front of a regiment in line on its own ground except by one or other of two complicated manoeuvres known respectfully as 'Countermarch on the centre' and 'Reverse the front by the wheel-about of troops'. The first, which could only be done at a walk, took at least five minutes to perform, whilst the second, which could be done at the trot, took nearly as long, whilst, in both, the smallest mistake on the part of the leaders would throw the whole regiment into inextricable confusion.

Chapter 4. *Note* 1

The period of these events was near the end of an era when all punishments ordered by higher authority were very severe – barbarous by present-day standards. It was a time when corporal punishment was accepted by the people as an established custom; punishments authorised by the civil authorities were no less barbarous than those in vogue in the services. On the other hand, it seems that corporal punishment was awarded on a grossly exaggerated scale for trivial misbehaviour and sentences varied considerably according to the whim of the Commanding Officer in some cases.

It is reasonable to say that the lash not only smashed a man's body but also his self-respect; to be effective as a deterrent both to the prisoner and the assembled watchers it had to be harsh and it had to be dramatic. The Duke of Wellington's sole recipe for discipline was flogging and death. In his latter years he reported to a Royal Commission:

'... I have no idea of any great effect being produced on British soldiers by anything but the fear of immediate corporal punishment ...'.

It is possibly one of the most marked flaws in Wellington's character that he should have possessed such a scarcely veiled contempt for the men he led to victory, saying:

'... they are the scum of the earth; English soldiers are fellows who have enlisted for drink – that is the plain fact, they have *all* enlisted for drink.'

In the Army tradition reigned supreme and the right to award corporal punishment was the symbol of traditional authority. Ignoring the fact that that which might kill the officer had to be lightly borne by the man in the ranks, the supporters of flogging asserted that '... nothing but the cat can bring the soldier to heel; he is of coarse clay; he understands it; he accepts it.'

Charles Napier, one of the best friends the men in the ranks ever had, pleaded passionately after Waterloo for the abolition of the cat except on active service. The agitation which had been very vocal in Parliament at the turn of the century was renewed; a protracted and determined struggle set in between the abolitionists and the floggers. Those Members of Commons who wanted to preserve flogging were the same people who grudged even a single penny to improve the soldiers' lot and so eliminate many of the evils which led to the flogging triangle.

A Royal Commission in 1836 limited the award of lashes by a General Court to 200, that by a District Court to 150 and that by a Regimental Court to 100. The slave-trade abroad was abolished in the middle of the nineteenth century through humanitarian outcry, but flogging continued to be the rule in the services long after the liberation of the Negro. It was only after a long and bitter struggle that corporal punishment was abolished by Parliament in 1881.

Chapter 4. *Note* 2
When a prisoner showed signs of collapse he would be examined by the Surgeon and brought to with restoratives, after which the punishment might or might not be resumed, according to the Surgeon's view. One writer of the period (Buck Adams, 1843) recorded that in twenty-four years' service he only saw one case where the Surgeon stopped the punishment. But in fairness to the surgeons it must be said that they acted thus rather than expose the wretched prisoner to being brought out a second time for the rest of his punishment when his back had partially healed.

Chapter 4. *Note* 3
It was the custom to brand a man permanently with the initial letter 'D' of the word 'Deserter'. Some regiments used a brass instrument with one end composed of a series of needle-points in the shape of the 'D'. Pressure on a lever made the points shoot forward so that they inflicted punctures in the skin corresponding with their shape. Often the instrument used was merely a needle stuck into a cork with which a crude 'D' was jabbed into the flesh, although in later years the march of progress brought a special spring-loaded device that was supplied by a firm in the Strand, London. They also provided a variant in the form of the letters 'B.C.' to denote a 'Bad Character'. When the marks had been made an indelible fluid was rubbed into them so that it remained a permanent marking.

Chapter 4. *Note* 4
Immediately before Victoria's accession the uniforms of the Army suffered a series of alterations, the mounted men in particular being loaded with fantastic head-dresses and other exotic trappings, elaborate slung-jackets, dolmans and pelisses, while the infantryman received a huge shako. Officers were clad in queerly shaped forage caps, and smothered in gold lace, often having to spend large sums out of their own pockets on clothing, this fact providing a sort of 'means test' on the would-be cavalry officer.

When all other lancer regiments changed into blue tunics the 16th (after vigorous protests) were permitted to retain their original scarlet tunics; thus they became the only lancer regiment in the British Army to wear red. It is reported that one colonel of the regiment was so keen on this aspect of his command that he did his best to enlist only men with red hair and mounted them only on chestnut horses! In parade uniform a 16th Lancer would be dressed as follows:

On the head a tall lance-cap of black, with a flat top ten inches square, the whole surmounted by a black cock's-tail plume drooping a full sixteen inches over the cap. The tunic was double-breasted scarlet, with nine buttons in two rows; blue collar and cuffs; seven-inch-long skirt with blue turn-backs. On the shoulders a flat brass chain-strap and a square plate with rounded corners (to protect the shoulders from sword cuts) – these plates made it impossible for the wearer to lie down on his side or back when wearing his tunic! From the cap, gold cord was draped down on to the chest and finished in ornate loops on the left breast. Tight, blue overalls, strapped beneath the highly polished wellington boots, had double gold stripes running down their entire length. Gold waist-belts and cross-belts, with a scarlet leather box in the small of the back and a purple leather sabretache with a blue cloth face dangling at the side, finished off the picture of perfection.

One would assume that red as a colour presented the most conspicuous target to enemy fire. Investigations of the period claimed that red was the most fatal colour whilst the least conspicuous was Austrian grey. These revelations prompted an officer at the time to write:

'Better to run the risk in red. of a rifle bullet, than to be shot by one's own people for wearing a foreign uniform!*

The same man very stoutly defended red by carrying out his own research; he claimed that at 1000 yards blue, black, grey and red were but faintly distinguished, although a white belt across the body made a man an instant target. He possibly overlooked the fact that the artillery of the period had an effective range of less than 800 yards whilst the musket did little damage over 250–300 yards!

Chapter 4. *Note* 5

It seemed that the Army paid more attention to the care of the horses than they did to the welfare of their riders. The mounts were always immaculate; their appearance justified the hours of daily grooming that they received; in return they were quite capable of performing a fifty-mile march in a single day. These long marches were a regular regimental parade attended by

*Passage from 'The Life of a Soldier' (quoted from *Old Times Under Arms* by C. Field; Wm Hodge 1939).

rigorous routine; failure to conform to it in the slightest degree brought the most relentless punishment.

After the first ten miles of the march there would be a fifteen-minute halt, during which the horse's mouth was washed out and a wisp of hay given to it. A further six miles were covered and a halt of thirty minutes allowed, when the harness was removed, the horses rubbed down and given a peck of corn. Remounting, the regiment would march another ten miles before halting for a further fifteen minutes to again wash out the horse's mouth and give a wisp of hay, this was followed by a further six miles when a two-hour halt was ordered and the horses given hay and a feed of corn. Then another ten miles with a fifteen-minute halt, and the last eight miles done without a stop. On returning to barracks the horses were tended before anything else was done and were given bran mash in cold weather, beans were thrown in as well.

Chapter 4. *Note* 6

It seemed that the whole purpose of the Army had become forgotten in a welter of bottomless formalism and stultifying ceremony. This was expressed in a mania for ornate and absurdly unsuitable uniforms displayed in prolonged public parades – to the neglect of the manoeurves and exercises necessary to train the soldier for war. The Army seemed to be drifting away from progress; it defended itself against change by glorifying the traditions of the past so that they became the obsolete foundations for the future. The present was being paralysed by the past.

The soldiers themselves were beginning to show many of the weaknesses and vices of the lifelong professional soldiery. This brought the fear that they might well become a military caste within the nation – sons born in barracks succeeding their fathers in the ranks.

Chapter 5. *Note* 1

Without greatly concerning the home Government, the Honourable East India Company were waging some small wars in India. Whilst a few minor campaigns could not greatly ruffle the placid manner in which the home armies existed, the Indian Army had not suffered to a like degree. This resulted in a very gradual and almost imperceptible military transformation. From this arose the nucleus of the forces that were to win the small colonial wars of the later Victorian era and which were to remedy in some part the marked professional and technical shortcomings that followed Waterloo.

These colonial wars were small-scale affairs but they were never child's play; on occasions they assumed the nature of a gamble between relatively easy victory and complete annihilation. Sometimes they were more a struggle against Nature and the climate than a military operation. Often it worked out that the military commanders and statesmen alike were rescued from disaster and disgrace by the private soldier's display of courage, fortitude and patience. Although casualties sometimes proved unexpectedly severe, these colonial battles were viewed by all ranks as exciting affairs that spelled freedom from the awful monotony of barrack life.

Chapter 5. *Note* 2

Throughout the Victorian epoch the desire and craving for active service formed a permanent and paramount characteristic of all ranks. To be prohibited from partaking in such military festivals was regarded as a signal mark of disgrace! Recorded conversations and correspondence of the period literally quiver with the desire to see active service; months of arduous campaigning seemed to leave the thirst totally unslaked.

The colonial wars were a most satisfactory opportunity for military distinction and warlike adventure – two qualities that the Victorian soldier seized with both hands. If your own regiment did not go overseas then the officers would frequently try very hard to get a transfer to the smaller colonial forces that were raised abroad and officered by the Regular Army.

In many ways this was an admirable trait; in those days battle was almost the sole way in which a soldier could be competently judged. These small colonial wars provided more than the mere gratification of military ambitions or the love of adventure. They left a permanent mark on both officer and man by giving each other an understanding of their respective strengths and weaknesses; they also provided a valuable education in the handling of men.

It would hardly have been possible to better this situation in the mid-Victorian era; these 'small wars' did not allow the defects of the cramping and narrow regimental *esprit de corps* to be seriously felt. In fact, with such small forces, this regimental spirit and feeling acted as a competitive spur; a small expeditionary force would be knitted together in a remarkable manner in the face of a more numerous and barbarous enemy. Under such circumstances, leadership was best based on experience, intuition and boldness, the morale of the troops being of the utmost importance; this balanced the obvious lack of intellectual power in the higher ranks.

Home soldiering was a slow poison which could paralyse even the most ambitious and strong-minded by routine and lack of outlet for individual enterprise and responsibility. Foreign soldiering counteracted this, although lesser men than the British soldier of the period might have been affected by the deadening quality of too many cheap victories.

Chapter 5. Note 3
This was the day of 'commission by purchase' – a system which lay at the root of many gross and often ludicrous incongruities. Apart from an honourable few, most of the officers who had so purchased their commissions came to regard the Army as their private property and 'treated their regiments as a lounge they had taken on lease'.

Wealthy men were able to get out of serving abroad, and even at home they managed to stay away from their regiments for many months on end. This meant that regiments going on active service were led by officers who knew nothing of the men under them; the regiment had to start learning everything on active service that they should have acquired in peace-time.

Until 1842, three years before the events related in this book, there were no regulations laid down concerning passage allowances for officers proceeding abroad without their regiments. Under such circumstances the officer had to make the best bargain he could for the cost of the passage.

In spite of the system many outstanding leaders had risen through purchase. Even the Duke of Wellington himself had purchased the earlier steps of his promotion so that he commanded a battalion at the age of twenty-five. It was a system that saved the country the cost of providing retiring allowances for officers. Being utterly illogical, iniquitous and indefensible, it commended itself heartily to those in charge of the Army's finances!

Some years after Waterloo a Royal Commission was appointed to look into the matter of commissions by purchase; the Duke of Wellington strongly defended the system to this body, saying:

'It is promotion by purchase which brings into the Service . . . men who have some connection with the interests and fortune of the country. . . . It is this circumstance which exempts the British Army from the character of being a "mercenary army"; it has rendered its employment for nearly a century and a half not only inconsistent with the constitutional privileges of the country, but safe and beneficial . . . three-fourths of the officers receive but little for their service besides the honour of serving the King.'

This last sentence may well have some substance when the following facts are considered:

An officer's first duty on being appointed was to spend sixty pounds or eighty pounds (roughly a year's pay) upon his outfit. This was the day of the extravagant uniform; of bewildering and expensive dress changes. They all ended in the same principle, that clothing should be as tight as possible and covered with as much gold and silver lace as possible; that the head-dresses should be of an extravagant height with still more extravagant plumes, and the shabraque and other saddlery adornments as ornate as could be conceived. George IV, the British monarch after Waterloo, looked upon his soldiers as so many dolls to be adorned according to his caprices. All these frequent changes had to be paid for by the officer himself, without regard to his means of supporting such costs. In addition he also had heavy subscriptions of many days' pay on entrance to the Officers' Mess, chiefly for the purpose of buying costly articles of mess plate, china and glass more suitable for display than for the sober use of Messes liable to sudden marches, embarkations and other damaging events.

Chapter 5. *Note* 4
In peace-time wives usually went abroad with their husband's regiment; even without active-service conditions they were usually exposed to hardship and privation. From the time of the Restoration down to the Crimean War some of the men's wives were even allowed to proceed with their husband on active service. The classic number allowed was six per company, or six per 100 men; lots were drawn to decide upon the favoured ones. Those who were left behind faced certain poverty and often existed only through charity or by public assistance.

On active service the trials of the women were severe; those who survived the ordeal were usually thoroughly inured to hardship and came of a hardy breed. British military writings tell of many tough and courageous soldiers' wives who trudged alongside their menfolk during Marlborough's campaigns and in the Peninsular.

Chapter 5. *Note* 5
The transport of troop horses presented great difficulties; horses are bad sailors and are nervous so that they suffer severely from close confinement at sea. When cavalry regiments were going on long sea voyages, such as when proceeding to India, they would leave their horses behind them. On arriving in India, the regiment would take over the horses of the regiment they were relieving or else purchase local mounts.

Chapter 5. *Note* 6
Smoking was forbidden on troopships for fear of fire. Memories of the trooper *Kent* were still recalled. This sailing ship of 1400 tons belonged to the East India Company, and in February 1825 she embarked at Gravesend for Calcutta with 637 people on board, including 364 officers and men of the 31st Regiment (1st East Surreys) and 130 of their wives and children. On the morning of the 7th March she was in the Bay of Biscay, labouring under a strong westerly gale with a heavy sea. Owing to this, a spirit-cask in the after hold broke adrift and an officer of the ship went down with a lantern to secure it. A heavy lurch caused him to drop the lantern and at the same time stove in the cask – in an instant the spirit caught fire and the after hold was ablaze. It was soon

evident that she could not be saved. There was gunpowder stowed forward in her, and when the fire reached this the *Kent* would be blown to pieces. There was nothing to be done but to abandon ship.

Providentially, a small 200-ton brig, the *Cambria*, arrived on the scene and for five hours in the raging gale went on the dangerous task of ferrying boatloads of survivors from the burning *Kent* to the little *Cambria*. Many were washed away and drowned, or crushed by wreckage – there were many forms of death on that terrible day. Dangerously low in the water, filled to bursting point with 533 survivors, the *Cambria* wallowed for three days on her way to Falmouth. In all were lost 54 soldiers, I woman and 21 children.

Chapter 5. *Note* 7
Cholera is a disease due to a virulent bacillus in the digestive tract which causes purging, muscular cramp and rapid collapse. It has an incubation period of from one to three days and it occurs particularly in India and China, but is endemic and epidemic in many tropical regions. The disease is water-borne and carriers may infect food; flies also can affect food. Epidemics spread very rapidly. The onset is rapid, with severe vomiting, muscle cramp accompanied by exhaustion; the temperature is subnormal and the pulse rapid and feeble.

In severe cases the patient may die in anything from three to twenty-four hours; on the other hand, there is often a stage of reaction with rapid improvement. Relapses may be fatal.

Chapter 5. *Note* 8
The town of Calcutta is situated on the east side of the Hooghley and extends along it for about six miles. The approach by the river from the sea is interesting, the Hooghley being one of the most picturesque of Indian rivers. Its most beautiful spots are in the vicinity of the city both on the side of which the city is built and on the opposite bank. The course of the river is somewhat devious, a distance of sixty miles by land taking eighty miles along the river. The water in many places washes into the land forming deep bays, sometimes bold jutting promontories which are clothed with oriental foliage and arrest the traveller's attention. Along the river are ghats or landing places. These consist of many steps, particularly where the banks are precipitous, and there is architectural taste displayed in the construction; the steps are wide with fine balustrades and pagodas are frequently built near them. Calcutta is thickly hidden by the clustering trees and the course of the river and it is on a level site which makes it impossible to be seen from the river until it suddenly bursts to view in all its Eastern splendour.

Chapter 6. *Note* 1
In India the range of temperature is great and the climate varied, notwithstanding its general tropical character. From October to April, six months of the year, the weather in the region of Calcutta is cool enough for Europeans, but the remainder of the year is rendered unpleasant and sometimes unhealthy by the heat and rains. At Calcutta the thermometer stands at about 66 degrees in January and rises to 86 degrees in April.

Chapter 6. *Note* 2
The muscle-play brought on by work or exercise produces heat that must be dissipated as rapidly and effectively as possible. But unless at the same time there is an equivalent increase in the rate of heat loss from the body the temperature of the whole body is bound to rise. Exhaustion supervenes when the body temperature reaches a dangerously high level. The limits of tolerance are reached in high temperatures if the heat stress is too severe or if heavy work is performed under such conditions. The body temperature will rise and the sweating mechanism may become fatigued so that sweat rate diminishes and then ceases.

Exercise at such a level is excessively fatiguing and can be continued, if at all, only by a very strong act of will; the higher conscious nerve centres force the muscles to continue working. The heated blood increases the number of heart-beats and respiratory movements and the nervous system is affected and fails to regulate the bodily functions properly with the result that metabolism proceeds at a more rapid rate and the 'fires of life' burn faster. With the rise in body temperature, the sweating mechanism becomes fatigued and, after decreasing, sweating will cease. Body temperatures will then rise more steeply to temperatures over 106°F, when heat-stroke can occur. In heat-stroke the heat-regulating mechanism of the body is overwhelmed and body temperatures rise up to 109°F. or even 110°F. Heat-stroke is a most dangerous condition and is frequently fatal. It can be precipitated by a lack of fluid balance and severe work under very hot conditions.

Chapter 6. *Note* 3
Even so, if the 16th Lancers had realised it, they were far better off than the troops in the permanent barracks further inland. When the rains set in towards the end of June the general health of the regiments became very bad; the hospitals were crowded with sick and there were a number of deaths from heat apoplexy, dysentery and various forms of liver disease.

The barrack conditions in India were so bad as to be most injurious to European troops. It is recorded that the buildings in the Calcutta area, whilst differing little from others elsewhere, were particularly bad. One in particular had a cemetery on either side of it, each of its two wells being within a few yards of these places. During the hot weather the water supply was extremely scanty; during the rainy season the surface water ran into the wells. Within a mile of the barracks was a pestilential swamp across which the prevailing winds blew directly on to the barracks during the hot season. Every regiment that had been so unfortunate as to be accommodated in these barracks for a long period of years had been decimated by some disease or other.

General Charles Napier constantly assailed the authorities with the wing of a model barrack, hoping thus to lead the government to authorise an extension to his improvements. But Lord Dalhousie forbade the completion of his superb barracks and the materials collected for building the other wing remained to rot on the ground.

In later years, after the period of this book, when Napier was Commander-in-Chief in India, he renewed his exertions, built model barracks and laid down the true principals on which they should be constructed. Again in vain – he was first thwarted and then stopped by Lord Dalhousie and the military board of India. When Napier, sick and in pain, returned to England he spent his last days writing *Indian Misgovernment* (1850) through which he sought to arouse public attention to the horrible system of barracks in India. In this book Napier wrote:

'The barrack sacrifices soldiers' lives and happiness to a callacious dishonest economy. I charge the court of directors, the military board of Calcutta, the government of Bombay with shameful negligence of the soldiers' safety; and with good warrant, because they disregarded my representations when a high position and great experience gave a title to attention. The Colaba Barracks and King's Barracks at Bombay have destroyed whole regiments. I walked through the men's sleeping rooms there *upon planks laid in water covering the floors*! At the Colaba Barracks the soldiers die like rotten sheep under the nose of the council. In the Bengal Presidency the barracks are extremely bad; but more pernicious still is the number of men crammed into them. Losses by battle sink to nothing compared with those inflicted by improperly constructed barracks and the *jamming* of soldiers – no other word is sufficiently expressive.'

The old warrior goes on to say:

'Long experience and consultations with men of science, medical men and engineer-officers have taught me that every barrack-room should, in hot climates, allow at least *one thousand cubic feet* of atmospheric air for each person sleeping in a room. This is the minimum; with less, insufferable heat and a putrid atmosphere prevail – death is the result. The soldiers rise at night feverish or in profuse perspiration, to sleep out on the ground amid damp exhalations. To do so when heated by an overcrowded room is death. Some may escape, or merely lose health, but to escape is the exception – the rule is death! The inhuman drain upon life, health and the public treasury constantly goes on. It kills more soldiers than the climate, more than hard drinking and one half of the last springs from discomfort – the despair caused by bad barracks.'

In the museum at the Medical Staff Mess at Millbank, London, was preserved a small notice-board which is instructive – on it is inscribed:

COOKHOUSE LATRINES WASH-HOUSE

It was brought from the barracks at Ahmednuggur – where the one building served for all three purposes!

Chapter 6. *Note* 4

Fresh out from England, the officers found much in India that disgusted them. Particularly because it was to have a personal aspect in that it affected their regiment was the manner in which replacements were provided to bring them up to strength.

In accordance with the usual custom when a unit was leaving India, those men who did not wish to leave were permitted to volunteer to other corps, and every effort was made by the authorities to induce soldiers to remain in India. All discipline was suspended, and the most disgraceful scenes of drunkenness were not only connived at but even encouraged during the weeks immediately before embarkation. Many men were inveigled by these discreditable means into volunteering to other regiments and to extend their Indian service without realising what they were doing. Such activities were going on in Calcutta at this time. A Light Dragoon Regiment were in the area awaiting return to England, having been in India since 1813, over thirty years. Lieutenant-Colonel McDowell was forced to fill the vacancies in the ranks left by the cholera victims from this source.

Chapter 6. *Note* 5

Much of the sickness among the troops in India could be blamed on to the abominable food they ate, both when provided by the Army and when purchased from private civilian sources. In both cases it was cooked in a filthy and disgusting manner. Even in the Officers' Messes (in those pre-railway days) it was difficult to get any food fit to eat. Dirty black boys acted as cooks, in some cases working outdoors amid dust and flies over a smoky open fire. Here they frizzled altogether in small earthenware saucers the lean goatsmeat, miscalled mutton, or stringy underfed buffalo, along with a few bad vegetabes that were supplied as rations.

There was one thing that all foreign stations had in common – cheap drink. This applied whether it brought profit to the Government by being sold in the canteens or whether it was brewed under indescribable conditions by natives. Using wood alcohol and berries to increase the potency of the liquor, these native-brewed drinks brought in their wake blindness, gastro-intestinal irritation and pain, unconsciousness and tetanic convulsions probably leading to death.

The efforts made by Henry Havelock in the mid-1830s to encourage temperance among the troops had only made a small impression upon the army at large. In the 13th Corps, of which Havelock was adjutant for some years, his efforts had succeeded in establishing a Temperance Society with a coffee-house to wean men from the wet canteen.

Chapter 6. *Note* 6
Later it was found that the smaller Arab horses were much more suitable for the country. But best of all were the local horses; country-breds who could stand up to the gruelling work. Admittedly, they were a menace in the horse-lines and brutes to ride out of the ranks, but neither Capes nor Walers could stand up to the hard work like the country-breds.

Chapter 6. *Note* 7
The twenty-one inch barrel carbine-bore carbines would have been a great asset to the lancers because with them they would have been able to defend themselves at longer range than was possible with their pistols. Pistols had been withdrawn from cavalry in 1840 but had been retained, for some unknown reason, by lancer regiments.

Chapter 6. *Note* 8
The drama that ended in the Sikh Wars began when the young baron, Ranjit Singh, at the age of seventeen, murdered his mother and hacked his way to power. By cunning, common sense, bribery and battle he overcame his rivals, and welded their loose confederacy into a single mighty army. He threw off the Afghan yoke and before he had reached the age of forty he was supreme throughout the Punjab; he had turned a sect numbering about half a million into the strongest nation in India. The Sikhs occupy the richly watered region of India known as the Punjab; it lies in a great triangle bordered by the River Indus and its tributaries. Correctly speaking, they are not a race but a numerous religious sect, originally a spiritual and peaceful brotherhood. Stimulated by repression and persecution, they transformed themselves into a powerful military group known as the Khalsa, or 'Saved Ones'. Not for the first time in history a religion became a military power as religious fervour was eclipsed by military zeal. The outward signs of their faith were the unshorn hair, the short drawers and the blue dress. The military nature of their calling being denoted by the addition of the affix *singh* or lion to the generic title of Sikh

or disciple. For the first time in India a nation arose, embraced all races, classes and grades of society, and banded together in the face of the foreign foe.

Every Sikh enjoyed all the privileges of Khalsa citizenship: exemption from taxation, freedom to oppress and liberty to live like a brigand. Although commanding an empire that stretched from the Khyber to the Sutlej and northwards over Kashmir, Ranjit Singh made no attempt to devise a system of government. There were no law-courts, no schools, no prisons – the only punishment were fines for the rich and the lopping off of a limb for the poor. He never made or repaired a road or bridge; the only works of public utility he constructed were forts – self-interest was the mainspring of all his actions and his vaults were crammed with cash and jewels.

The almost legendary figure was a man of small stature with a single eye which looked droll in his pox-pitted, puckered face. He had a habit of retiring to debauchery when diplomacy failed. Surrounded by beautiful Kashmir girls, he inflamed and stupefied his nerves with a mixture of raw corn-spirit, opium mush and the juices of raw meats. His excesses caught up on him eventually and at the age of fifty he was old and frail, white-bearded. Unable to walk unaided he refused to give up riding; he would step on to the neck of a kneeling attendant, who would slowly rise to transfer his master on to the back of the waiting horse. Through a seizure he lost the power of articulate speech but made himself understood and cowed all round him by a series of guttural grunts.

Ranjit Singh had long known that his domination was a one-man affair and that his children (half-brothers many of them) were incapable of maintaining what he had built. Polygamy is the curse of dynasties; there are few enemies in the East like the sons of one father but with different mothers – half-brothers are deadly menaces. In the well-conducted Asiatic kingdoms the man with the noose was sent round to attend the half-brothers at the time of accession! After the Old Lion had gone his reign of tyrannous law and order ceased; crimes, assassinations and wholesale massacres became daily events in the Punjab; no one was strong enough to seize power with sufficient popularity to hold it. There came a series of intrigues, murders and kidnappings reminiscent of the Italian courts of the Middle Ages, from which finally emerged the young Maharajah, Dhulip Singh. He was ruled over by the Rani, his ambitious mother (called by Sir Henry Hardinge 'the Messalina of the East'). She was aided by her current lover, Lal Singh, who with Tej Singh commanded the Army. On the sidelines was a powerful nobleman, Ghulab Singh, waiting to see which way the cat jumped.

The Khalsa were dominating the Punjab through its Panchayets, or military committees. The two Army Commanders, Lal Singh and Tej Singh, decided that their only chance for power, and indeed survival, was to break the power of that army. They could think of no better method than to throw them against the British bayonets; recent British reverses in Afghanistan had resulted in lowered prestige. They were aided by the ever-recurring Sikh fear that the British were planning to annex the Punjab; each little indication or movement of the British furthering that fear. Finally a unique situation arose in which an army was encouraged to go to war whilst its commanders were in constant communication with the enemy, 'assuring them of their support and cooperation at all times'!

Chapter 6. *Note* 9

Sir Henry Hardinge arrived in India in July 1844 to succeed Lord Ellenborough as Governor-General. He was sent with the express intention of preserving the peaceful state of the country. Almost at once he encountered a situation in the Punjab which rendered eventual warfare almost inevitable. The country was in a distracted condition, with its large army clamouring for pay and plunder. The Sikh court was split into factions by murderous intrigues that might well result in the Khalsa, the formidable Sikh Army, becoming sufficiently powerful to decide to invade British territory. The Sikh court remained in this dangerous state of flux throughout the early months of 1845. Throughout this period the Governor-General remained strictly on the defensive, indicating '. . . that nothing could be done by us to suggest that the internal affairs of the State of Lahore are matters for our concern'.

Nevertheless, he cautiously strengthened his frontier forces as much as possible and in such a way as not to give cause for the Sikhs to fear aggression. The nearest town to the threatened area, Ferozepor, had its garrison brought up to 10,000 men with some twenty-four guns under the command of a very reliable General, Sir John Littler. At both Ludhiana and Ambala he had between 8000 and 12,000 men with a considerable amount of artillery, and he brought up to Meerut a force of about 10,000 men with twenty-six guns. The force at Ambala was to be strong enough to move on Ferozepor, where Sir John Littler's force was obviously of insufficient strength to hold the Sikh army without waiting for the force from Meerut.

Although it was by no means certain in the minds of the British that the Sikhs would actually transgress and cross the River Sutlej into British territory, they were ready for the emergency if it occurred. Sir Henry Hardinge is reported to have said:

'When I hear of a single piece of Sikh artillery having crossed the Sutlej I shall consider the movement to have been in earnest.'

Sir Hugh Gough, the Commander-in-Chief of the British Armies in India, concurred and observed:

'I am still of the opinion that they will never be beaten on this side of the river, except as plunderers.'

Chapter 7. *Note* 1

March orders for a cavalry regiment of the period on the move in India (actually entered in the diary of a 16th Lancer) read as follows:

'The Commanding Officer having observed great irregularity on the line of march begs the strictest attention to be paid to the following orders: No man on any pretence is allowed to leave the ranks until the trumpet sounds "Halt". An N.C.O. of the troop is to remain with the men and when the column resumes its march they are to rejoin the Regiment at a steady pace, which is on no account to exceed a trot. Officers are held responsible that their men do not ride in a slovenly or unsoldierlike manner, any man persisting in such conduct is to be dismounted and made to walk the remainder of the day's march.'

Chapter 7. *Note* 2

Marching-out strength on parade was 28 officers, 501 N.C.O.s and men and 546 troop horses; in addition there was the usual innumerable horde of camp-followers. The officers had to find their own tents and transport. There were 25 horse-keepers and 60 grass-cutters allowed officially to each troop, and the tents were carried by 28 elephants, 45 camels and 40 mules. Altogether there were something like 10,000 men, women and children – and the column on the road was over six miles in length.

Chapter 7. *Note* 3

The diseases of India are numerous, but at this time the most dangerous was Indian Cholera Morbus. India was thought to have been the birthplace of this pestilence, but there is reason to think that its first incidence might well have been in Persia. Its virulence was increased by the crowded state of British Army camps and barracks and its intensity increased in damp areas; troops camped in small numbers in high and dry country suffered comparatively little.

H. T. Princep, accompanying the army commanded by Lord Hastings in 1817, wrote graphically of the sufferings of the men during an epidemic of cholera:

'This army, when first seized, was encamped in a low and unhealthy part of Bundelkund, on the banks of the river Sinde, a confluent of the Jumna, which has its source in the mountains of Malwa. The year was one of scarcity, and grain had been collected for the troops, through the camp-followers, with extreme difficulty, and of course of inferior quality. The water of the country, except where it could be obtained from running streams, was indifferent. The time of the year too was that at which the heat of the day is most strongly contrasted with the cold of the night. To all these extraordinary circumstances was superadded the very crowded state of the camp of so large an army. For about ten days that the disease raged with its greatest fury, the whole camp was an hospital. The mortality amounted to about a tenth of the whole number collected there. The narrator himself lost seven domestic servants and a moonshee in about four days, besides twelve others who were sick and unserviceable for a month, out of an establishment of fifty-three; and others of the staff were equal sufferers.

'Europeans and natives, soldiers and camp-followers, were alike affected; but the latter being generally worse clothed and fed than the fighting men, suffered in a greater proportion. Of the Europeans fewer were seized, but those who took the disease more frequently died, and usually within a few hours. The camp was abandoned, and the army continued for some days to move to the eastward, in the hope of finding relief in a better climate; but each day's march many dead and dying were abandoned, and many more fell down on the road, - so many that it was not possible to furnish the means for carrying them on, although the utmost possible provision had been made by the previous distribution of bullock-carts and elephants for the accommodation of the sick. Nothing was heard along the line of march but groans and shrieks and lamentations; even the healthy were broken in spirit and incapable of exertion; and, for the time, the efficiency of this fine army seemed to be entirely destroyed. Towards the end of November, when the army reached a healthy station at Erech, on the right bank of the Betwa river, the epidemic had visibly expended its violence.'

In the fifty-seven years preceding the Indian Mutiny the annual rate of mortality amongst the European troops in India was sixty-nine per thousand, and in some stations was even more appalling. In 1864 there was a Royal Commission appointed to inquire into the sanitary conditions of the Army in India. They discovered, for example, that in most cases the only efficient scavengers and refuse collectors around camps and barracks were the huge birds of prey called adjutants. So great was the dependence placed upon the exertions of these unclean creatures that the troops were warned that any injury done to them would be severely punished. The Commission piously expressed the hope that by taking the proper precautions the mortality might be reduced to the rate of twenty per thousand per annum. This hope was realised and it is recorded that since 1882 the annual death-rate among British troops never rose as high as seventeen per thousand.

Chapter 7. *Note* 4

The horrible birds never left them during the epidemic, but followed daily on the march, not as guardian angels but as loathsome scavengers who could pick a body to pieces in a very short time. It became a point of honour to deny these birds their prey and not a man died in the regiment without being given the final gratuity of a shallow grave in the hard earth.

Chapter 7. *Note* 5
The real situation was as follows:

On the 12th of December 1845, half in tumult and half in awe, the Sikh Army had surged forward over the river Sutlej and into British territory. Here they had halted in solemn dread at their own temerity; they had broken the treaty and crossed the dividing line that separated them from the mighty power that had struck down empires!

The British agents in Lahore, the Sikh capital, had been sending intelligence reports denying that such an event would ever occur, so that the British were somewhat astonished at the turn of events. It had never, in spite of their reluctant readiness, been seriously visualised that such an operation would ever take place. The British had expected a more drawn-out civil-type of operation against which a strong counter-thrust and a few un-strenuous battles would result in the much underrated Khalsa being thrust back over the river into the Punjab.

Sober official British despatches termed the invaders as a 'rabble', whereas in reality the Sikh soldiery were to be the most stubborn fighters encountered by the British during their entire period in India. Their infantry were trained to the highest degree of efficiency by European mercenary officers and their superbly drilled gunners worked the heaviest artillery in the entire country. If the British disparaged them the native soldiers in the Company's employ greatly feared the Sikh forces. It is to be considered a fortunate occurrence that the tactics of this well-trained native army were to be modified by the involuntary awe that they felt for the British Army's reputation in the East.

Chapter 7. *Note* 6
The Sikh Army, the Khalsa, were not only large in number but were very well trained and equipped. Dedicated and stimulated by religious zeal, their manoeuvres and firing were brought by the training of their European mercenary officers to be equal to that of the British troops and infinitely superior to that of the Company's native sepoys. These white officers had been imported by the Old Lion, Ranjit Singh; realising that it was his people's nature to fight, he had employed these scattered fugitives from the Napoleonic Wars to bring his armies to the point of being the most efficient fighting force on the entire continent. Many of the officers were French and possessed Napoleon's love for heavy artillery, consequently they equipped the Sikh Army with twelve- and eighteen-pounder guns, of which they had over 300, served by excellent artillerymen who could fire very rapidly and accurately. All words of command were given in French.

During his lifetime Ranjit Singh had carefully kept free of open struggles against his white neighbours; he realised that his dreams of power necessitated either fighting or making friends with the British and he wisely preferred the latter course. But on his death in 1839, urged on by many advisers for their own ends, the Khalsa contemplated trying their strength against the white soldiers and the native levies of the Company. One of the first actions of the successors of Ranjit Singh was to sack the foreign officers and few if any of them were in command of Sikh units immediately prior to, or during, the Sikh Wars.

The infantry wore either a red turban, red coats with black belts and yellow facings, and white trousers, or black tunics with yellow facings and white cross-belts, light blue trousers with a red stripe and a loose yellow turban. The cavalry wore a steel helmet in the shape of a turban, a red coat with black belt, white trousers and jackboots. They had much the same arms as the British – muskets, swords and pistols. There were also hordes of irregular cavalry available known as Ghoorchurras. They were dressed in loose yellow silk garments, many of them wore chain mail and round polished steel helmets, surmounted with heron plumes.

Chapter 8. *Note* 1
The army by which the territory of British India was garrisoned, defended and by which its wars had been conducted, consisted of three elements. These were the Queen's troops, the Company's troops and the contingent troops of the native states. The Queen's troops were conveyed to India at the Company's expense and whilst in the country were given extra pay from the same source. The Company's own army consisted of two distinct types of troops – European and native; the latter were dressed in the same scarlet as the British soldier so that they would better impress the armies of the native states by their likeness to the actual line infantry of Britain. The British troops were brigaded with the native regiments; it was noticeable that success attended the operations of British and sepoy units when they were amicably co-operative. Similarly, lack of success followed when such comaraderie was missing.

Because of lack of organisation and possibly inadequate command the Army in India was not, at this time, a machine from which the best results could be expected. It was not easy to mobilise it on a businesslike footing; its troops were not really trained as an army for war; and the troops, their commanders and their staff were, for the most part, untrained in their war formation. The supreme military authorities appear to have had little organisation and carried casually on with the work of preparation for a campaign. Because of these circumstances the men in the ranks had to suffer heavy losses in the desperate fighting required to regain the advantage thrown away by the want of competent heads and eyes to lead them. In the forthcoming battle with the Sikhs hundreds of men were to meet their deaths storming batteries of guns because their masters had not provided the artillery to silence them.

Nevertheless, in spite of these deficiencies, it was this Indian army with its British core that defeated the warlike and numerically superior Mahratta and Sikh armies in the first part of the nineteenth century. After the Indian Mutiny in 1857 the Army of Bengal was disbanded, whilst the Armies of Madras and Bombay were blended into the Queen's forces without such a drastic purge.

Chapter 8. *Note* 2
During Sir Charles Napier's conquest of Sind, in 1845, an incident occurred that has since been commemorated in a poem by Sir Francis Doyle, 'The Red Thread of Honour'.

It was necessary to reconnoitre the interior of a deep pass at Truckee by ordering a party to scale the exterior rock wall. For this purpose a part of the old 13th, veterans of Jellalabad, was sent up the mountain; the ascent, long and arduous, was all but completed when it was observed from below that the flat top of the rock held a strong force of the enemy, entrenched behind a breastwork of stones. The ascending body of the 13th numbered only sixteen men, the enemy on the summit was over sixty. In vain the officer who made this discovery tried to warn the climbers of the dangers so close above them, but which they could not see; his signs were mistaken by the men for fresh incentives to advance, and they pushed on towards the top instead of retracing their steps to the bottom. As eleven men of the small party gained the summit they were greeted by a matchlock volley from the low breastwork in front, followed by the charge of some seventy Beloochees, sword in hand. The odds were desperate; the 13th men were blown by the steep ascent; the ground on which they stood was a dizzy ledge, faced by the stone breastwork and flanked by tremendous precipices. No man flinched; fighting with desperate valour they fell on that terrible but glorious stage, in sight of their comrades below, who were unable to give them help. Six out of the eleven fell at once; five others, four of them wounded, were pushed over the rocks, rolling down upon their clambering comrades who had not yet gained the summit. How hard they fought and died one incident will tell. Private John Maloney, fighting amid a press of enemies, and seeing two comrades, Burke and Rohan, down in the mêlée, discharged two muskets into the breast of a Beloochee, and ran another through with his bayonet. The Beloochee had strength and courage to unfix the bayonet, draw it from his body, and stab Maloney with his own weapon before he himself fell dead upon the rock. Maloney, although severely wounded, made good his retreat and brought off his two comrades. So much for the fighting on both sides. Now for the chivalry of those hillmen. When a chief fell bravely in battle it was an old custom among the clans to tie a red or green thread around his right or left wrist, the red thread on the right wrist being the mark of highest valour. When that evening the bodies of the six slain soldiers were found at the foot of the rocks, rolled over from the top by the Beloochee garrison above, each body had a red thread not on one one wrist but on both.

Chapter 8. *Note* 3
The Commander-in-Chief of the Queen's forces in India was also Commander-in-Chief of the Company's army, whilst the officers of that army were appointed by the directors. Because of the age at which they became colonels and majors, not one in fifty of the Company's officers were able to stand the wear and tear of an Indian Campaign. After about a fortnight in the field they were said to be a burden to themselves, an annoyance to those under them and a terror to everyone but the enemy.

Promotion among the officers went by seniority and, despite the havoc wrought by the climate, was very slow. Subalterns frequently waited fifteen years before they became captains and any man of the grade of colonel was likely to be past his work; whilst a general was sure to be too old and worn out for active service. This slowness of promotion made a regimental career unsatisfactory to a young man and many of them sought employment in the political branch. Among those who followed such a course were such men as the Lawrence brothers, James Outram and Nicholson – the 'politicals' were probably the ablest men in India. But such a weeding out of their best men left the Indian regiments with those who were perhaps idle and inferior, but who could be relied upon to show daring and reckless courage without necessarily leading their men in an intelligent fashion. However, many were good soldiers, excellent as subordinate commanders, but quite unfit for supreme command and paralysed when called upon to assume responsibility and display initiative. Sturdy courage and obedience to instructions was a characteristic of these men, who were the most reliable assets in the Army – as long as their limitations were known and recognised.

Chapter 8. *Note* 4
An army on the move over the plains of India resembled a mobile city; a community in which the combatants numbered only about 15 per cent of the population. Because leave to England (other than sick leave) was not gained until after ten years' service the officers settled down to make India their home; in peace-time they lived comfortably in cantonments with a host of servants; in war the sallied forth with huge amounts of personal kit and

attended by their servants. In the Afghan War of 1839 one brigadier required sixty camels to carry his personal baggage; the army that marched to Seringapatam in 1799 moved in a hollow square with a front of three miles and a depth of seven miles with intervening spaces containing 120,000 animals of all types ranging from the elephant to the ass!

Even on this march from Meerut to Ambala some of the officers required six camels to carry their baggage, although they were told before they left that all they would need in the field would be their canvas bed, a tent, a blanket, a second pair of breeches, a second pair of shoes, half a dozen shirts, a second flannel waistcoat, a pair of towels and a piece of soap. As it turned out, many of them lost much of their impedimenta through camels dying or camel-drivers deserting.

Chaper 8. *Note* 5
A camel will die of practically anything; in this case they perished partly from neglect and partly through being fed on a type of grain that did not suit them. These losses did not begin until later in the march because the early stages were comparatively easy. This was due to the foresight of Major Broadfoot, the Political Officer, who had moved heaven and earth (including the use of force where necessary) to establish a series of food dumps on the route. Coupled with the ample water supplies and the abundance of firewood from the dense jungle that lined the road, the men and beasts fared reasonably well in the first part of the march.

But towards the end, as was usual on such marches, the route was marked by the dead beasts left by those who had just passed by. Each of these animals had been tended to the last by its driver, for his own sake and for the sake of the valuable load – it was not abandoned until it was obvious that it could go no further.

Chapter 8. *Note* 6
There was very little chance of purchasing food from the few villages through which they passed, most of them were deserted or the food hoards hidden. It is not easy for those who are unacquainted with the East to fully appreciate what the march of an Indian Army, with its thousands of camp-followers, means to inhabitants of the country being traversed. The effect upon the districts passed through was very like that caused by the march of a huge column of locusts before they can fly. The walking locusts go forward in the direction they have fixed upon, turning neither to right nor left, eating up as they advance every green leaf in their path, leaving an absolute desert behind them. Such was the result of the march of an Indian army through the districts of India.

Chapter 8. *Note* 7

The whole action at Mudki on the 18th of December 1845 was unsatisfactory and unduly costly. Gough threw his tired men at well-disciplined and prepared troops who were partly hidden with their heavier artillery in the jungle. In the face of an Asiatic enemy boldness is a great virtue and to fly at the Sikhs as soon as he found them was not, in principle, unsound tactics for Gough to follow.

Although a muddled and perhaps indecisive victory. Mudki was notable for the bravery of the British soldier and the lack of heart shown by the native sepoys of the Company's army – casualty figures indicating that the bulk of the work fell upon the British soldier.

The losses were 215 killed and 655 wounded, made up as follows:

Personal Staff	2 officers killed	2 wounded
General Staff	1 " "	1 "
Artillery	27 killed	47 "
Cavalry	81 "	87 "
Smith's Division	78 "	339 "
Gilbert's Division	18 "	100 "
McCaskill's Division	8 "	79 "

Sir John McCaskill and Brigadier Bolton were killed, gallant old Sir Robert Sale, the Quartermaster-General, died from the effects of a grapeshot wound, Herries, the son of the Cabinet Minister, and Munro, two admirable staff officers, were killed, and Hillier was severely wounded, as were Brigadiers Wheeler and Mactier and Major Pat Grant, the Deputy Adjutant-General of the Army. Also killed were 13 European officers and 2 native officers.

In the Cavalry Division the 3rd Light Dragoons, who took 497 men into action, suffered most severely – losing 2 officers, 56 men and more than 100 horses killed, with 35 men wounded – mostly as the result of charging against guns in battery. The native Cavalry lost 1 officer and 20 men killed, 6 officers, 1 native officer and 43 men wounded. Among the infantry, the bulk of the fighting had fallen upon Sir Harry Smith's Division; in this formation H.M's 31st Foot lost 156 of all ranks; H.M.'s 50th Foot lost 125 of all ranks; and the native corps 136 of all ranks. The 47th Native Infantry, which were brigaded with the 31st, did not have a tenth as many casualties as the European regiment. General Gilbert's Division lost 118 of all ranks. In McCaskill's Division the only officer killed was its commander; H.M.'s 80th Foot had 24 casualties; H.M's 9th Foot 52 casualties and the native regiments only 11 casualties between them.

The Sikh losses were severe, the ground being littered with their dead and wounded; seventeen of their guns were captured or destroyed.

Part of the British losses must be ascribed to the courage and fanaticism of the Sikhs; their gallantry and discipline during the fighting evoked admiration from the British troops. Brave as they were, they expected no mercy and gave none; they killed and mutilated the wounded and even when the life of a wounded Sikh was spared, in many instances they turned and fired into the backs of their deliverers. So strong was the indignation among the 3rd Light Dragoons, horrified at finding their wounded comrades cruelly murdered, the 'Remember Mudki' became a battle-cry and many Sikhs were ruthlessly slain who would otherwise have been spared.

Chapter 8. *Note* 8

The list of casualties from the battle shows not only how stubborn was the fighting but also how the brunt of it was borne by the British troops. Out of 2415 casualties, 1207 were Europeans, including 115 officers.

'Our native cavalry did not behave well,' wrote Hardinge a week later. 'The 3rd Dragoons on every occasion behaved admirably, going through everything . . . the British infantry as usual carried the day. I can't say I admire sepoy fighting.'

Sir Hugh Gough had one horse killed under him, and Lieutenant Frederick Haines, one of his personal staff, was severely wounded. The Governor-General had every member of his staff disabled, and Major Broadfoot was killed, together with Arthur Somerset and Brigadier Wallace. General Gilbert had one horse killed and another wounded under him; and Brigadiers Harriott, White and Taylor were all wounded. The heroes of the action were probably the 3rd Light Dragoons – it is rare for cavalry to charge entrenched infantry and artillery, and only troopers of rare devotion and discipline would have faced such a trial. The 3rd had lost nearly 100 men and over 120 horses at Mudki only two days before; they lost 152 more men and 60 more horses on the 21st, yet the remnant without hesitation charged and defeated superior numbers of Sikh cavalry on the 22nd.

The total losses were:

Killed:	Officers	(British)	37	Men	(British)	462
		(Native)	17		(Native)	178
		Total:	694			
Wounded:	Officers	(British)	78	Men	(British)	1054
		(Native)	18		(Native)	571
		Total:	1721			

Grand total of all ranks killed and wounded: 2415.

Sikh losses during the battle were originally given by Sir Hugh Gough as 100 guns and probably 5000 killed and wounded – as the Sikhs had only 88 guns, including those brought up by Tej Singh, it is also reasonable to assume that the figure of their casualties is likewise exaggerated. Cunningham reports that Sir Hugh learnt after the war that the loss of the Sikhs in killed probably amounted to 2000 in all, as the heirs of 1782 men of the regular troops alone claimed balances of pay due to the relatives of the slain. This points to great slaughter, but, as Cunningham vaguely indicates, it was a common remark at the time that very few Sikh dead were to be seen on the field after the action.

Of the British infantry, the heaviest loss fell upon the 9th, who had 280 casualties; the 62nd 260; the 1st Europeans 204; the 29th 184; the 31st 142; the 50th 124 and the 80th 81. Thus, in two actions separated by only three days, the 9th had suffered over 330 casualties and the 31st close upon 300. The native regiments which suffered the most at Ferozeshah, as at Mudki, were the 2nd and 16th Grenadiers.

Nearly 700 of the dead were buried beside the church at Ferozepor. The Duke of Wellington, writing to Sir Hugh Gough on receipt of the news of the battle, and lamenting the heavy losses, said:

'Long experience has taught me that such achievements cannot be performed without great loss, and that in point of fact the honour acquired by all is proportionate to the difficulties and dangers met and overcome.'

The writer had once lost a third of his army at Assaye; the Ferozeshah casualties did not exceed one-eighth.

Chapter 8. *Note* 9

Without a shadow of a doubt General Sir Hugh Gough was a very brave and gallant man, but men of such calibre often lack imagination and foresight – therein lies their courageous strength because they cannot foresee that what they are doing might be dangerous to them. During his earlier campaigning days Gough had acquired a long white coat (probably of reversed sheepskin) which he was in the habit of donning when action threatened – 'so that all should see me'. The white coat played a conspicuous part both at Mudki and at Ferozeshah; at the latter battle, on the second day, Gough was most moved at seeing his gallant soldiers forced to hold their ground under an intense cannonade from heavy Sikh guns. His emotions became overpowering and, accompanied by his aide-de-camp, the Hon. C. R. Sackville-West, the gallant old man in his conspicuous white coat rode off at an angle in front of his troops to draw the Sikh fire upon himself. Shot fell all round the two men but neither of them moved nor were they touched. The sight of the brave old man (he was then more than sixty-six years of age), sitting there in his white fighting coat, greatly cheered his troops; he was a man much loved by the men in the ranks who saw nothing strange in Gough's fiery habit of flinging infantry in with the bayonet against artillery in prepared positions.

When later charged by critics with exposing himself beyond the actual call of duty Gough said:

'Those about me may have thought me reckless – my own feelings were utterly different from that.'

The famous white coat can now be seen on display in the National Army Museum at Camberley in Surrey.

Chapter 9. *Note* 1
This was one of the first occasions on which it is recorded that the fierce little hillmen from Nepal took part in operations with the British.

The two battalions of Gurkhas greatly distinguished themselves in the hard-fought battle of Sobraon, shortly after Aliwal. It was said that without their sterling performance the British attack might well have failed.

Chapter 9. *Note* 2
Sir Harry Smith was the most dashing leader in the Army, loved by his men because he never needlessly risked their lives or asked them to do anything that he would not do himself. He was a gallant and courageous soldier who had served continuously in the British Army since 1805. As a rifleman, he had fought in the Peninsular, South and North America, South Africa and India. He had shown great courage at Mudki and Ferozeshah, although approaching his sixtieth year, and was definitely a man to be admired.

Charlie Cureton was a 16th Lancers officer although he had never actually commanded the regiment, joining them in 1819 after a remarkable career which had begun in 1806 in the Militia. In the tradition of the time he was a wild youth and soon got into deep debt, so deep that he was in danger of being committed to a debtors' prison. When he disappeared, leaving his clothes in a bundle on the beach, it was assumed that he had drowned himself rather than face that final disgrace. In reality he had disguised himself as a sailor and sailed for London, where, under the name of Roberts, he enlisted in the 14th Light Dragoons. He fought throughout the Peninsular War in the ranks, had his skull fractured by a sabre cut at Fuentés d'Onor and in 1814 was given a commission in the 14th Light Dragoons for gallantry in the field. He then reverted to his own name and later transferred to the 16th Lancers; he had acquired a great reputation as a dashing cavalry leader when serving under General Gough in the Gwalior War.

Chapter 9. *Note* 3

The arrival of the heavy guns from Delhi had an interesting sequel. The long column marched into the British camp on the 7th and 8th of February 1846, the sepoys gazing with delight at the long array of stately elephants dragging the huge and cumbersome ordnance.

The Sikhs had constructed a position of strong earthworks and deep ditches in a half-circle backing on to the river at Sobraon; it presented a formidable problem even with the artillery reinforcements. At seven o'clock on the 10th February, after a delay caused by heavy mist, the encircling British guns opened up.

Old Sir Hugh Gough, a man of action rather than of letters, found that the barrage aroused in him a feeling almost of poetry, for in his official despatch he wrote:

'Nothing could be conceived grander than the effect of the batteries when they opened. As the cannonade passed along from the Sutlej to Little Sobraon, in one continuous roar of guns and mortars; while ever and anon, the rocket, like a spirit of fire, winged its rapid flight high over the batteries in its progress towards the Sikh entrenchments.'

For more than two hours the cannonade thundered its way back and forth across the battlefield, the Sikh guns valiantly responding. Then the British fire began to slacken; the ammunition for the heavy guns was nearly expended. This news was brought to Sir Hugh Gough, who showed no sign of alarm or hesitation. To the surprise of the officer who had brought the message, Sir Hugh's face lit up as he cried:

'Thank God! Then I'll be at them with the bayonet!'

Chapter 10. *Note* 1

Investigations carried out during the earlier part of the nineteenth century seemed to indicate that marching under the Indian sun was perhaps not so detrimental to the health of the soldier as was thought. But when one delves further into these reports it is found that they were conducted under peace-time conditions and that they stress the importance of the soldier having his clothing adapted to the climate, his head properly protected, and his arms and accoutrements lightened. Few if any of these precautions prevailed during the period of the Sikh War. With such measures in mind it was suggested that more men were lost by night marches than by those conducted *with suitable care* during the hottest part of the day.

During the Indian Mutiny of 1857 General Havelock's forces in their marches and counter-marches whilst relieving Cawnpore and Lucknow were claimed (by General Havelock) to have suffered no injury through exposure to the weather. General Wilson during his command of the forces besieging Delhi reported that the troops had better health then when in barracks.

Knowing the condition of these buildings and bearing in mind that while on active service the troops were probably deprived of excessive amounts of drink, such a situation is not surprising!

Chapter 10. *Note* 2
The actual weight and quantity of the kit carried by the men themselves was said to be incredibly great, every variety of article being heaped on the saddle, which was a heavy wooden-treed concern with a projecting wood cantle that hurt the small of the back when a fence was jumped. The personal equipment of a lancer included a so-called 'lassoo equipment', picket-peg, head-and-heel ropes, and heavy iron shackles in addition to the steel collar chain and 'pioneer equipment'. This meant that a lancer in full marching order weighed an average of twenty-three stone, and a packed saddle required two men to lift it on to a horse's back!

Chapter 10. *Note* 3
This fact, coupled with the cutting off of some of the rearguard and baggage by Sikh cavalry, led to a spate of rumours flying alarmingly back to the Army of Smith's baggage being totally lost. The 16th Lancers lost their hospital stores among the other baggage, the men amused themselves hoping that the Sikhs would drink the medicines thinking them to be wine! The 16th Lancers' officers lost their entire baggage and all the Mess kit, including a quantity of plate; in those days everything used in cantonments was taken on the march.

The unlucky young officer who had been on baggage-guard, and only provided with four men, came in with a few things during the night and was promptly placed under arrest by the incensed Brigadier – nor did his misfortunes end there, because he broke his arrest to go into action with the regiment a few days later and was killed in the battle.

Chaper 10. *Note* 4
Many of the prisoners were treated fairly well by the Sikhs and returned after the battle of Sobraon. Those men who fell into the hands of the Sikh regular regiments were reasonably treated by them, but unhappily this was not extended to the sick and wounded, who were all murdered without mercy, perhaps by the camp-followers and villagers, as they lay in their dhoolies. Writing a day or so after the march, Lieutenant Robertson of H.M.'s 31st Foot Regiment:

'After two or three days we returned to Badawal, as the Sikhs had retired to the banks of the sutlej, and we found our poor sick men lying killed in the jungle, most of them in their dhoolies as they had been shot as they lay in bed, the muzzle of a musket being put against their side. You can imagine how savage the men were after such a sight.'

The bodies of these unfortunates were buried by their comrades on the 24th January.

Chapter 10. *Note* 5

If the Sikhs were prevented from being aggressive by the impending junction of Sir Harry's force with that of Colonel Godby from Ludhiana they were backing the wrong horse. Nothing at all had been seen of this force and frequent scanning of the horizon did not show any signs of dust-clouds denoting their presence.

In addition to his two-hourly messages Sir Harry had sent Lieutenant Holmes with a party of Irregular cavalry to inform Godby at daybreak that he had been forced to change the direction of his march. Soon afterwards he sent off Lieutenant Swetenham of the lancers, and a short time after that Lieutenant Bond-Smith of the engineers – all these officers reached their destination. Knowing that Godby was aware of the enemy anticipating him, Sir Harry was reasonably justified in expecting some co-operation or demonstration in his support; Godby had been repeatedly and urgently asking that the force should advance to his relief prior to their being attacked. Lieutenant Holmes found that Godby was only just turning out and his force did not actually move off from Ludhiana until 8 a.m. when the firing had commenced and then they had eight or nine miles to travel to make contact. At the time Sir Harry was not to know this and his manoeuvres were necessarily cramped since he felt obliged to refrain from any deviation of route as it might make the junction of the two forces even more difficult. As it transpired. Godby moved off late, then took the wrong route because he failed to assess correctly the changed march that the force was following, and eventually returned to Ludhiana after a fruitless jaunt across country – without firing a shot!

Chapter 10. *Note* 6

The Sikhs appear to have derived considerable satisfaction from this skirmish, which they blew up to the magnitude of a major action, although it only caused 21 killed and wounded and 19 captured to Her Majesty's 31st Regiment, whilst the 53rd Regiment had 36 killed and 12 wounded; the native regiments coming off far more lightly.

Chapter 11. *Note* 1

Nearly 400 infantry were missing at the end of the march, but more than 200 straggled in during the next twelve hours. The 16th Lancers had got off incredibly lightly – only having 2 men killed and 1 wounded.

Chapter 11. *Note* 2
At first Sir Harry had considered attacking the Sikhs at Badowal, and his force rested and prepared for the battle. But Runjoor Singh showed sound judgement in evacuating the place and marching northwards, towards the river where he was reinforced at the Tulwun Ghat, eight miles lower down the Sutlej, by 400 regular infantry of Avitabile's corps, twelve guns and some cavalry. Throughout, Runjoor Singh had shown a reasonably high standard of generalship, enough to cause Sir Harry to respect him sufficiently to plan his battle thoroughtly. The Sikh Commander had been particularly astute in posting himself at Badowal, threatening both Smith and Godby like a king between two pieces on a draughtboard – Sir Harry reckoned this to be the most scientific move made during the whole war, whether by accident or design. In spite of not forcing home his attack at Badowal, Runjoor Singh had handled his troops well, although his cavalry could have given the British a great deal more trouble than they did. But the Sikh cavalry, unlike their infantry and artillery, was never very effective.

Chapter 11. *Note* 3
Sir Harry Smith had no intention of pursuing the same bull-at-a-gate tactics employed at Mudki and Ferozeshah, by throwing his smaller forces against entrenched Sikhs with strong artillery. It would seem that Smith jumped at the opportunity of having a separate command with which he could justify his recorded criticisms of the tactics employed in the two previous battles. Trained under the Duke of Wellington and Sir John Moore, he coupled a vast military experience with extreme bravery and impetuosity. His handling of this latest task amply qualified him as a commander equal to any in India at that time. In a campaign not exactly noted for its high tactical standards, Sir Harry Smith had a guiding star . . . 'I steered the course invariably pursued by my great master, the Duke, never needlessly to risk your troops or fight a battle without an objective.'

Chapter 11. *Note* 4
Back at the main camp they had heard of the loss of Smith's baggage-train and highly magnified versions of his casualties were being bandied around. The subsequent cries of disaster and woe causing both the Commander-in-Chief and the Governor-General to tremble for the safety of the precious siege-train and ammunition convoy. The Governor-General was most anxious that Ludhiana should be relieved and, riding down into Gough's camp in the middle of the night, requested him to reinforce Smith at once. Gough ordered out the 2nd Brigade of Smith's Division under Brigadier Wheeler, who had recovered from the wound he had received at Mudki. This was formed of

Her Majesty's 50th Regiment, the 48th Native Infantry and Sirmoor Gurkhas, together with two regiments of Native Cavalry (one of which was the Governor-General's bodyguard) and four Horse Artillery guns. They left on the 22nd January and arrived at Dharmkot on the evening of that day. Continuing the march on the following day they reached Sidham after a heavy journey of fifteen miles, where it was discovered that a large force of Sikhs were between them and Smith's force. Wheeler now showed the same lack of resolution that was to cost him his life at Cawnpore eleven years later during the Indian Mutiny. He decided to return to Dharmkot and move round on a circuitous route to Jagraon. The weary force arrived back at Dharmkot at 6 p.m. after thirty miles under very hot sun and through heavy sand, without even having time to cook their rations.

The 50th Regiment might well have felt that their luck was deserting them; the whole campaign for them had been hard and unfortunate and they doubtless grumbled loud and long before sinking into fatigued sleep on that night of 23rd January 1846. In the first place they had arrived at Ludhiana on the 7th December 1845, where they had been inspected by the Governor-General on the 11th December, who told them that they would soon be employed. He had stopped near the colours of the regiment and told their Commanding Officer, Colonel Ryan, that he hoped his men would behave as he had seen the old 50th do in the Peninsular. Bridling, the Colonel had replied: '. . . that they were only anxious to be tried.' Orders had been read out on the evening parade on the 13th December directing the regiment to hold itself in readiness to march next morning, but further orders would be issued if they were actually to proceed. This further order was issued at about 11 p.m. and sent to Colonel Ryan, who was living some distance from the camp. He sent an orderly up to the camp with it at once, but the messenger seemed to have made some mistake about delivering it, with the result that the 50th did not parade at daybreak on the 14th, as it should have done, and the rest of the brigade marched off without them! They started off at about 8 a.m. in a state of confusion, but soon overtook the native infantry regiments of the brigade near the fort of Badowal, which was taken without resistance. Some companies of the native infantry took possession of the fort and four brass guns, which were at once sent off to Ludhiana in charge of four companies of sepoys.

After the capture of Badowal, Lieutenant Brockman, who in the hurried departure of the regiment had come without baggage, went back on foot for it. He must have been captured by the enemy because he was never heard of again. Two other officers who went back at the same time on horseback rejoined in safety, having seen nothing of him. Two British prisoners were afterwards reported by spies to be detained in the enemy's camp, and one of these it is supposed might have been Brockman; but nothing further was ever heard of him, and he was eventually struck off the strength of the regiment by a court of inquiry – being reported 'Killed in passing Wadni'.

The brigade had then marched to Basseen, which was reached at sunset without halting, after a fatiguing march of over thirty miles on heavy sandy roads. No tents or baggage came up until the following morning so a poor night was spent by all. Similarly unpleasant marches followed for the next few days, culminating in their dinner being disturbed by the battle of Mudki, where they lost 125 men killed and wounded, both their colonels having their horses shot from under them. They were depressed by the death of the Roman Catholic priest of Ludhiana at Mudki, where he went into action with the regiment – his body being brought in dreadfully mutilated after the battle. At bloody Ferozeshah they lost another 129 officers and men during a hard day's fighting, and a fearsome night in the midst of the enemy when they had to fight their way back at least a mile in the blackness of the night. They felt their luck had changed when they realised that Corporal Hale of the Light Company and Private Johnson of the Grenadiers had captured two enemy standards and Sir Harry Smith had shown his evident pleasure with them. But now the luck seemed to have swung back to bad again and they were a quiet, dispirited bunch who trudged into Sir Harry's camp at Ludhiana on the 26th January.

Chapter 11. *Note* 5

As a result of another one of the Governor-General's forays into the Commander-in-Chief's camp, Brigadier Taylor was ordered to move on the 27th to Dharmkot, and the Shekawati brigade from Basseen to Jagraon. There was some discussion about this, as the Commander-in-Chief felt that Sir Harry Smith was being given enough men to take Lahore, but Sir Henry Hardinge pointed out to him, with the aid of a map, that this would mean the enemy positions being menaced from three points, and he acquiesced. Considering his force adequate to defeat the slightly larger Sikh force, Sir Harry Smith sent a messenger to the Commander-in-Chief that he would not require Taylor's force. This might well have caused a lesser man than Hugh Gough to mutter: 'I told him so!' as he recalled his argument with Sir Henry Hardinge on the subject.

Chapter 12. *Note* 1

The Indian battalions, like the Europeans, had scarlet coatees and white cross-belts, white drill-covered shakoes which some brigades had discarded as the weather grew cold. The British infantryman with his ammunition carried about fifty-six pounds (including three days' biscuit ration in the haversack). The weight was made up by the accoutrements: knapsack, canteen, camp-kettle, blankets, greatcoat and clothing.

Chapter 12. *Note* 2
Brigadier Cureton had split his cavalry force up into two brigades, one of which was commanded by Lieutenant-Colonel McDowell of the 16th Lancers. This meant that at Aliwal the 16th were commanded by Major J. Rowland Smyth.* A contemporary note says of him: '. . . he was a splendid horseman and a keen rider to hounds. A tall man, his shoulders broadened and his waist narrowed by the exaggerated cut of his superb scarlet jacket. His face, framed by the peak of his lance-cap and the golden chin chain, was ruddy, with a long straight nose above a bushy but well-trimmed moustache; his eyes were clear and penetrating.'

Chapter 12. *Note* 3
The infantry were still armed with the old 'Brown Bess' musket of the Peninsular War which weighed about twelve pounds, had a calibre of 0.753 inch, the diameter of the bullet being 0.68 inch; the bullets weighed fourteen and a half to the pound and the infantryman carried sixty rounds of ball ammunition in his pouches. The extreme range of these muskets was in the region of 400–500 yards, but their effective killing range was usually about 100 yards, but only with controlled fire by volleys. Therefore the greater the concentration of men who were able to fire at one time, the better the chances of hitting the enemy. The ritual drill words of command, some of which survive to this day, ensured that the battalion or regiment brought their maximum fire-power to bear at the same time. Marksmanship was not aided by the dense cloud of smoke which hung over the battle-field and reduced visibility to as little as seventy or eighty yards. It was possible for a trained soldier to load and fire three times in a minute but he could expect two out of every thirteen shots to be misfired; veteran soldiers could probably manage four or even five shots a minute but the recruit was not in the same standard and would often forget to remove his ramrod before pressing the trigger thus reducing his rate of fire to nil, at least until he acquired another ramrod. But even to fire three shots a minute it was necessary for the soldier to have a fairly good flint in his musket, a clean priming pan, dry powder and a barrel that was not unduly fouled by gunpowder so that ramming was made difficult. Furthermore, owing to the complicated operation that was necessary in order to reload, this could only be done by standing up. Each time the musket was loaded, a ramrod had to

*From *History of the 16th, the Queen's Light Dragoons (Lancers)*. Henry Graham (1912).

be pushed down a forty-two-inch barrel. As this was often topped by a wicked-looking triangular bayonet with a seventeen-inch blade, this was frequently made very difficult; it is probably a fair assumption that fixed bayonets halved the rate of fire.

Chapter 12. *Note* 4
It is worth remembering that the Horse Artillery only possessed light pieces throwing six- or nine-pound shot. With these, they were engaging on equal terms the heavier Sikh guns that fired twelve- or eighteen-pound balls. The British gunners could probably maintain a rate of fire of about two shots in one minute with their lighter pieces. The cannon had to be laid afresh after each shot because there was no means of checking recoil action. Ranges were estimated by the gunlayer or captain and thus the extreme practicable range was confined to the limit of the human eye, roughly one thousand yards, on a clear day; but in battles of this period the day was rarely clear. So that gunners could see their target, plus the fact that the missile had a flat trajectory, it was essential that the guns took post in front of their own infantry, otherwise there was a risk of the shot ploughing into the backs of their own men. Loading these pieces was attended by certain dangers especially if the barrel was not properly swabbed to extinguish any glowing particles of powder or wadding before ramming home the next charge. In order to minimise the danger of a blow-back the first command in the reloading sequence was 'Stop your vent' whereupon number 3 of the crew placed his thumb, protected by a leather-stall, over the touch-hole and kept it there until the fresh charge of wad had been placed home. Charred thumbs were another of the occupational hazards of a number 3 whose thumb-stall often cracked and burnt through during a prolonged engagement.

These field-pieces fired ball for long-range work and this type of solid shot often ricocheted as much as four or five times on hard or stony ground. It is recorded that at Waterloo a ball fired from a distance of some 600 yards was seen to mow down a file of seventeen men, ricochet, plough into the side of a British square of infantry and finally bounce out on the other side. Even when the shot had lost initial velocity, it was still dangerous when merely rolling along the ground – this was demonstrated to a British line infantryman who casually put out his foot to stop such a ball and had his foot carried away. The two short-range projectiles were canister, which contained a large number of ordinary musket balls which tended to fan out from the muzzle, and grapeshot, which was composed of rather heavier balls mixed with small pieces of scrap metal. Although the spread was not as wide as canister, the stopping power of grapeshot was greater and it was used with great success against cavalry.

The British had always been specialists with Horse Artillery, their teams so impressed the French during Napoleonic Wars that in 1818 they paid us the compliment of setting up a special committee to study our horse artillery, men, horses and equipment.

Chapter 12. *Note* 5
Writing afterwards about this charge a man of Captain Bere's squadron said:

'They gave us a volley at forty yards, a ball from which struck the chain of my lance-cap just over the left cheekbone. I was into them by then, and delivered a point at one fellow but could not quite reach him, and was about to settle a second when a blow from a sabre from behind severed my arm just above the wrist, and my hand, grasping the lance, fell to the ground. Not being able to make my horse break the ranks, I slipped my feet out of the stirrups and endeavoured to throw myself off. In doing this my sword belt caught the cantle of the saddle, but fortunately, the belt broke, and I found myself on the ground. I lay for a few moments reflecting on what I should do, when a ball came within a few feet of my head, which at once convinced me that this was no place of safety. On getting up to make my way to the rear I was met by a Sikh who, seeing my helpless condition, placed his musket within a yard of my head. Just at that moment I lifted my arm as though to strike him, and fell forward to the ground. He fired, and his charge burnt a portion of the hair off the back of my head, the ball entering my left shoulder. I lay for a few moments expecting the cowardly rascal to finish me with his bayonet, but while he was reloading, an artilleryman came up and gave him the contents of his pistol, but as this only wounded him, he dismounted and ran him through with his sword. After this I got up and grasping the stump of my right arm, again made for the rear. I had not gone far before I found myself in front of a troop of our artillery, who were only waiting for our squadron to get out of the way before opening fire on the retreating enemy. I managed to get between two of the guns and then bolted as fast as I could, walking on for about a mile when I met with a doctor, who applied a tourniquet to my arm and gave me a glass of brandy-and-water. He directed me to a field hospital where, on arriving in a very exhausted condition, it was found necessary to amputate my arm just below the elbow.' The writer of that letter recovered and returned to England, he was invalided out of the army and granted the munificent pension of thirteen pounds per annum!

Chapter 12. *Note* 6
Brigadier C. R. Cureton rose to be Adjutant-General of Queen's troops in India. He was commanding a cavalry division during the Second Sikh War in 1848 and was killed at Ramnuggar when

shot through the heart by a matchlock ball whilst with his old corps, the 14th Light Dragoons. It was particularly tragic that this brilliant cavalry commander should have lost his life in a fruitless attempt to prevent a disastrous and foolish Balaclava-like charge.

Chapter 12. *Note* 7
Captain Pearson had been given a command of a wing of the 16th Lancers held in reserve, but on seeing the regiment go forward could not restrain himself and led his men into the attack!

Chapter 12. *Note* 8
In battle, troop horses, as long as they feel the hand of their rider and his weight on their backs are, even when wounded, singularly free from fear. But once deprived of his rider the troop-horse becomes crazed with terror. He does not gallop out of the action and seek safety; trained to range himself in line, he seeks the companionship of other horses, and mad with fear, eyeballs protruding, he attempts to attach himself to some leader, or to force himself into the ranks of the nearest body of riders.

Chapter 12. *Note* 9
These squares were really equilateral triangles, when one side was attacked the other two sides faced inwards and fired indiscriminately on any men who broke into the formation, without considering their comrades in the slightest. This partly accounted for the heavy losses of the 16th for most of their dead at this stage fell inside the squares. Indeed, no one who was wounded or whose horse fell had the slightest chance of escape if inside the square, as he was hacked to pieces instantaneously by the Sikh swordsmen.

Chapter 12. *Note* 10
An account of this part of the action by Sergeant Gould of 'C' Troop says:

'When we got out on the other side of the square our troop had lost both lieutenants, the cornet, troop sergeant-major and two sergeants. I was the only sergeant left. Some of the men shouted: "Bill, you've got command! They're all down!" Back we went through the disorganised square, the Sikhs peppering us in all directions. One of the men had both arms frightfully slashed by a Sikh, who was down under his horse's hooves and made upward cuts at him.'

Corporal F. B. Cowtan wrote afterwards:

'As for myself, I went through cavalry and infantry squares repeatedly, at the first charge I dismounted two cavalrymen and on retiring we passed through a square of their infantry, and I left three on the ground killed or wounded. One fellow was taking deliberate aim at me when I put my horse at him, and just in time, for his priming blackened my face. Sergeant Brown was riding next to me and cleaving everyone down before him with his sword when his horse was shot under him, and before he reached the ground he received no less than a dozen sabre-cuts, which of course killed him. My comrade on my left, just as we cheered before charging, had his heart torn from his side by a cannon-ball, but my heart sickens at the recollection of what I witnessed that day. The killed and wounded alone in my squadron was forty-two.'

Chapter 13. *Note* 1

Owing to the loss of all their hospital supplies during the Badowal march, the 16th's surgeons were working under considerable difficulties, but Surgeon Burt aided by Currie and Stevens did their best for the many casualties sustained by the regiment. The Commanding Officer, Major Smyth, was found to be severely hurt by a bayonet thrust through the waist, the weapon having broken off and remained in the wound but, notwithstanding the intense pain he suffered, he would not allow the surgeons to dress him until his men were attended to. From the position of the wound it seemed impossible that he would recover, but fortunately the point of the bayonet had carried with it a large piece of cloth and a portion of his sword-belt, and these seemed to have pushed the bowels aside in the abdominal cavity without injuring them. Major Rowland Smyth was in splendid health and training and was off sick list in six weeks!

Chapter 13. *Note* 2

It is hard, in this day and age, to conceive the terrible plight of the wounded men in these colonial wars of the nineteenth century. They lay helpless under the blazing sun for hours, unable to move and praying to be discovered and picked up. But even if this occurred in time to do much for them, the primitive surgery of the day conducted under the most appalling conditions resembled more the activities of a torture-chamber rather than a hospital.

If, on the other hand, the battle was lost they could expect nothing but murder and mutilation from their savage foes or, worse still, to be handed over to the women. Being the gentle sex, their methods were not so sudden as the impact of their husband's broad-bladed spear or blunted scimitar, they favoured fixing the wounded man's mouth open with a stick and, crouching over him, urinating until he drowned.

Aliwal was a relatively small, compact battle, fought over a definite area and ending long enough before darkness fell to enable some of the wounded to be brought in. But after other battles it was not unusual for a man to lie helpless for perhaps two or three days and nights, maybe on a slope with his head downhill. During this time, if he was lucky, he might be visited by a comrade or a soft-hearted civilian touring the battle-field to succour the wounded, and given a drink; possibly moved in a mistaken attempt to help him, so that the clotted wounds broke open and he bled to death. But on the 28th January 1846 the wounded were fortunate, the water-carriers toured the battle-field, going from one shattered man to another, to be followed by teams of bearers with dhoolies in which the injured man was to be carried to hospital. Tender and gentle as they probably tried to be, the untrained Indian bearers gave the wounded men their first foretaste of the horrors to come as they bundled them into the unpadded litters and jerkily bore them over the rough ground off the battle-field.

Chapter 14. *Note* 1
When they were first brought in the pale helpless soldiers lay on the ground, on blankets, old overcoats and bits of clothing; with bloody rags bound around heads, arms and legs. The odour of blood mixed with the fresh scent of the evening. Some had limbs shot clean off by roundshot, others bullets through breast or abdomen; some had indescribably horrible wounds in the face or head. All were mutilated, sickening, torn, gouged out; some were mere boys, others were wrinkled-faced veterans of many campaigns who had suffered all this before. The attendants were few and overworked; the wounded whatever their condition patiently waited until their turn came to be taken inside. The litters and dhoolies arrived in clusters and one after another left behind their stricken load; returning to the field for more. The men generally made little or no fuss, whatever their sufferings; all that was heard were a few groans that could not be supressed and an occasional scream of pain as they lifted a man from the ground or took him from a dhoolie. The sufferings of the men on the litters were not entirely the fault of the Indian bearers; the rough and littered condition of the terrain caused them to roll their bleeding burdens about; lack of training caused them to put their litters down with an unco-ordinated bump when they needed a rest, on some occasions almost throwing the patient off. When moving on the actual battle-field it was necessary to pick their way through the Sikh wounded in very careful fashion because, even in near-death, these warriors would try to hamstring or wound anyone who came near to them; these were occurrences which did not help to give the patient a gentle ride.

Darkness came, and in the tents and in the open spaces around where the wounded had been brought, the surgeons were working desperately by candlelight and moonlight. The misty field of pain replaced the field of battle, and on it death was a subtle antagonist, not always in a hurry. A man who was carried to a field surgery for treatment in the 1840s underwent the worst experience of his life; frequently the last experience. If he had a mortal would such as a musket-ball in the intestines, he would be immediately passed over because there was no hope at all for him and treatment was merely a waste of precious time; when an arm or leg was badly smashed, the accepted remedy was amputation – without anaesthetics. It has been charged that limbs were often needlessly sacrificed by the surgeons; that they were particularly fond of amputating and were just as likely to amputate for a flesh wound as for a fractured bone. This was claimed on the grounds that they could do it more quickly than they could dress the wound; that it made a neater job, thus gratifying professional pride. It was undoubtedly true that many flesh wounds were so ugly that the only real safety for the patient lay in amputation. He was taken in charge by surgeons who had their bare arms and grubby aprons smeared with blood, their knives held between their teeth while they stood back and waited for the patient to be laid on the table, or else helped him to get into the desired position. The man's teeth grated as he ground them together to avoid crying out; his face was drawn and pallid with pain, he tried to lift his head to see his trousers ending at the ankle in a bloody tatter and a stump.

'A roundshot, eh?' said the Surgeon. 'No use trying to save that leg, you must have it off at once, my man, at the knee.!

He called to a sweating orderly:

'Here, lend a hand, hold this man down for me while I amputate – take my flask, fill the poor devil up with rum first.' He reached for his saw.

The operation took place upon boards put on two trestles, which were not particularly satisfactory; during the three-minute operation the man had to be supported in his writhings by the orderly's arm underneath and another orderly on the other side grasping his wrist. When he had finished the Surgeon would wipe his bloodstained saw and knives across his apron a couple of times; according to the medical customs of the time he was not particularly fussy about cleanliness, the principles of asepsis being unknown. His tools were few and resembled a carpenter's kit; he had no specialised instruments, no hemostatic forceps, retractors, hypodermic syringes or even a clinical thermometer – his only means of estimating a fever were by touching the patient's brow. In fact, the best surgery of the day could probably have been done by competent butchers or carpenters, because speed of operation was the vital factor, thus minimising the shock element.

The hastily stitched-up stump was sometimes plunged into a tub of hot tar or pitch to cauterise the wound and seal the ends of the severed vessels. The more up-to-date surgeons might know the method of ligaturing the vessels with silk strings, the ends of which would hang out of the stump, those tying major vessels being identified by having knots tied in them. After a few days the unknotted cords were pulled to see whether or not the tissues had rotted away sufficiently to allow them to come loose. When the knotted strings were similarly pulled, after a longer period, a gush of blood would follow showing that the vessel had not healed. If this happened then the wound would have to be re-opened and the vessel tied higher up or even a further amputation carried out. If a soldier were lucky and had a strong constitution he might come through it with only the loss of the limb, but many things could go wrong within a few days. The complete lack of antiseptic precautions brought many dangers in its wake. Human flesh is very vulnerable without modern safeguards and gangrene was a frequent and highly dangerous accompaniment to his other sufferings.

A surgeon of the day wrote:

'Often did I see a simple gunshot wound, scarcely larger than the bullet which made it, become larger and larger until a hand would scarcely cover it, and extend from the skin downward into the tissues until one could put half his fist into the sloughing wound.'

An amputee might appear to be going along nicely with his wound freely discharging the 'laudable pus' that contemporary surgeons thought a favourable sign. Suddenly the wound would dry up, the man become more feverish with increasing pain – he had blood-poisoning, a death sentence, for only three out of every hundred recovered when that occurred.

During the Sikh War both sides were using muskets which fired a bullet about 0.68 inch in diameter, and weighing fourteen and a half to the pound. This soft-lead ball, travelling at relatively low velocity, was likely to spread upon impact, shatter bones and leave a dreadful hole in a man – a wound far removed from the neat holes made by modern steel-jacketed bullets. Even a shoulder wound, today sometimes counted as a blessing and a 'Blighty' wound, was a terrible affair. The ball would make a small hole where it went in, but in smashing through the bones of the shoulder would spread and tear a tremendous hole where it came out, partially exposing the shoulder-blade. Such a wound would still be open and discharging freely twelve months later, and the shoulder would be completely ankylosed and the arm entirely useless. Then years later would find general weakness of the whole joint with considerable muscular atrophy or wasting – the train of disability and suffering went far into the future for the wounded soldier 120 years ago.

When the frightful operation had mercifully ended, the man did not really leave the site as the theatre was merely a part of the wards; it was not screened off in any way. He would be laid a few feet away, on a dirty blanket spread on the ground, wrapped in a blanket or greatcoat still with blood and filth, his head on his boots. Only a few yards away outside the ward there would be a growing heap of amputated feet, legs, arms and hands. Several dead bodies would lie near, each covered with a brown blanket. Later, some fresh, shallow graves, mostly for officers, would be dug in the soft ground; broken boards or barrel staves were stuck in the ground, inscribed crudely with their names. It is recorded that ten years later, after the battle of Balaclava in the Crimea, piles of arms and legs, with the sleeves and trousers still in them, had been thrown into the harbour and could be seen dimly through the water. Bodies of dead men would rise suddenly and horribly out of the mud to the surface and anchor chains would be fouled by limbs and trunks. The surface of the once translucent water was covered with brightly coloured scum and the whole village smelt of sulphuretted hydrogen.

Such scenes of horror were nothing new in British military annals, similar miseries had been materially assisted by the attitude of the officer towards the private soldier many times before. The officers were fantastically courageous and physically tough, but they regarded the men they commanded as denizens of another world. Lord Raglan, for example, who was later to command in the Crimea, had his arm amputated without anaesthetics after Waterloo and had called out: 'Here, bring that arm back; there is a ring my wife gave me on the finger.' Savage physical suffering was born by both officers and men alike, it had always been the case. Far worse miseries were endured outside Quebec during the winter of 1759, during the retreat to the Ems in 1797. In the disastrous Walcheren expedition of 1809 a whole army was lost through sickness; men died in their thousands in the hospitals of the Peninsula. It must be remembered that if the fighting methods and the uniform had not altered since those days, neither had the medical treatments. Demands for clean bedding, soup and hospital clothing were considered preposterous luxuries and highly unreasonable. Evidence given to the Hospital Commission, examining the terrible state of Crimean hospitals at Scutari in 1854, said:

'I served throughout the whole of the Peninsular War. The patients were never nearly so comfortable as they are here . . . In general the men were without bedsteads. Even when we returned to our own country from Walcheren and Corunna the comforts they got were by no means equal to what they have here.' And even the schoolboy is aware of the hospital conditions encountered by Florence Nightingale in the Crimea.

Appendix 1

STRENGTH OF TROOPS UNDER
MAJOR-GENERAL SIR H. SMITH, G.C.B.

		Officers and men
Artillery – Major Lawrence:		
Horse Artillery (six-pounders)	22	
3rd Artillery (nine-pounders)	6	
Shekawati Brigade	4	
Total Artillery		32
Cavalry – Lieutenant-Colonel Cureton –		
1st Brigade (McDowell):		
16th Lancers	530	
3rd Light Cavalry	372	
4th Irregulars	398	
		1300
2nd Brigade (Steadman):		
Bodyguard	351	
1st Cavalry	422	
5th Cavalry	402	
		1175
(Major Foster):		
Shekawati		631
Total Cavalry		3106
Infantry – 1st Brigade (Lieutenant-Colonel Hicks):		
31st Regiment	544	
24th Native Infantry	481	
36th Native Infantry	571	
		1596

2nd Brigade (Lieutenant-Colonel Wheeler):		
50th Regiment	494	
48th Native Infantry	857	
Sirmoor Gurkhas	781	
	——	2132
3rd Brigade (Lieutenant-Colonel Wilson):		
53rd Regiment	699	
30th Native Infantry	824	
Shekawati Brigade	781	
	——	2304
4th Brigade (Lieutenant-Colonel Godby):		
47th Native Infantry	713	
Nussaree Gurkhas	586	
	——	1299
Total Infantry		7331
Sappers		28

Appendix 2

Major-General Sir Harry Smith, K.C.B., to the Adjutant-General of the Army

Camp, Field of the Battle of Aliwal, Jan 30, 1846

Sir,

My despatches to his Excellency the Commander-in-Chief of the 23rd* instant, will have put his Excellency in possession of the position of the force under my command, after having formed a junction with the troops of Loodiana, hemmed in by a formidable body of the Sikh army under Runjoor Singh and the Rajah of Ladwa. The enemy strongly entrenched himself around the little fort of Budhowal by breastworks and 'abattis', which he precipitately abandoned on the night of the 22nd instant (retiring, as it were, upon the ford of Tulwun), having ordered all the boats which were opposite Philour to that Ghat. This movement he effected during the night, and, by making a considerable detour, placed himself at a distance of ten miles, and consequently out of my reach. I could, therefore, only push forward my cavalry as soon as I had ascertained he had marched during the night, and I occupied immediately his vacated position. It appeared subsequently he had no intention of recrossing the Sutlej, but moved down to the Ghat of Tulwun (being cut off from that of Philour, by the position by force occupied after its relief of Loodiana), for the purpose of protecting the passage of a very considerable reinforcement of twelve guns and 4000 of the regular, or 'Aieen' troops, called Avitabile's battalion, entrenching himself strongly in a semicircle, his flanks resting on a river, his position covered with from forty to fifty guns (generally of large calibre), howitzers, and mortars. The reinforcement crossed during the night of the 27th instant, and encamped to the right of the main army.

Meanwhile, his Excellency the Commander-in-Chief, with that foresight and judgment which mark the able general, had reinforced me by a considerable addition to my cavalry, some guns and the 2nd Brigade of my own Division, under Brigadier Wheeler, C.B. This reinforcement reached me on the 26th, and I had intended the next morning to move upon the enemy in his entrenchments, but the troops required one day's rest after the long marches Brigadier Wheeler had made.

*Not received by the Secret Committee.

I have now the honour to lay before you the operations of my united forces on the morning of the eventful 28th January, for his Excellency's information. The body of troops under my command having been increased, it became necessary so to organise and brigade them as to render them manageable in action. The cavalry under the command of Brigadier Cureton and horse artillery under Major Lawrenson were put into two brigades; the one under Brigadier MacDowell, C.B., and the other under Brigadier Stedman. The 1st Division as it stood, two brigades:– Her Majesty's 53rd and 30th Native Infantry, under Brigadier Wilson, of the latter corps; – the 36th Native Infantry, and Nusseree battalion, under Brigadier Godby; – and the Shekawattee brigade under Major Forster. The Sirmoor battalion I attached to Brigadier Wheeler's brigade of the 1st division; the 42nd Native Infantry having been left at headquarters.

At daylight on the 28th, my order of advance was – the cavalry in front, the contiguous columns of squadrons of regiments, two troops of horse artillery in the interval of brigades; the infantry in contiguous columns of brigades at intervals of deploying distance; artillery in the intervals, followed by two 8-inch howitzers on travelling carriages, brought into the field from the fort of Loodiana by the indefatigable exertions of Lieutenant-Colonel Lane, Horse Artillery; Brigadier Godby's brigade, which I had marched out from Loodiana the previous evening, on the right; the Shekawattee infantry on the left; the 4th Irregular Cavalry considerably to the right, for the purpose of sweeping the banks of the wet nullah on my right, and preventing any of the enemy's horse attempting an inroad towards Loodiana, or any attempt upon the baggage assembled round the fort of Budhowal.

In this order the troops moved forward towards the enemy, a distance of six miles, the advance conducted by Captain Waugh, 16th Lancers, the Deputy Assistant Quarter-Master of Cavalry, Major Bradford of the 1st Cavalry and Lieutenant Strachey of the Engineers, who had been jointly employed in the conduct of patrols up to the enemy's position, and for the purpose of reporting upon the facility and point of approach. Previously to the march of the troops it had been intimated to me by Major Mackeson that the information by spies led to the belief the enemy would move somewhere at daylight, either on Jugraon, my position of Budhowal, or Loodiana. On a near approach to his outposts, this rumour was confirmed by a spy, who had just left the camp, saying the Sikh army was actually in march towards Jugraon. My advice was steady; my troops well in hand; and if he had anticipated me on the Jugraon road I could have fallen upon his centre with advantage.

From the tops of the houses of the village of Poorein I had a distant view of the enemy. He was in motion and appeared directly opposite my front on a ridge, of which the village of

Aliwal may be regarded as the centre. His left appeared still to ooccupy its ground in the circular entrenchment; his right was brought forward and occupied the ridge. I immediately deployed the cavalry into line, and moved on. As I neared the enemy the ground became most favourable for the troops to manoeuvre, being open and hard grassland. I ordered the cavalry to take ground to the right and left by brigades; thus displaying the heads of the infantry columns; and as they reached the hard ground I directed them to deploy into line. Brigadier Godby's brigade was in direct echelon to the rear of the right; the Shekawattee infantry in like manner to the rear of my left; the cavalry in direct echelon on, and well to the rear of both flanks of the infantry; the artillery massed on the right and centre and left. After deployment, I observed the enemy's left to outflank me, I therefore broke into open column and took ground to my right. When I had gained sufficient ground, the troops wheeled into line. There was no dust, the sun shone brightly. These manoeuvres were performed with the celerity and precision of the most correct field day. The glistening of the bayonets and swords of this order of battle was most imposing; and the line advanced. Scarcely had it moved 150 yards when, at ten o'clock, the enemy opened a fierce cannonade from his whole line. At first his balls fell short, but quickly reached us. Thus upon him, and capable of better ascertaining his position, I was compelled to halt the line, though under fire, for a few moments, until I ascertained that, by bringing up my right and carrying the village of Aliwal, I could with great effect precipitate myself upon his left and centre. I therefore quickly brought up Brigadier Godby's brigade; and, with it, and the 1st brigade under Brigadier Hicks, made a rapid and noble charge, carried the village, and two guns of large calibre. The line I ordered to advance, – Her Majesty's 31st Foot and the native regiments contending for the front; and the battle became general. The enemy had a numerous body of cavalry on the heights to his left, and I ordered Brigadier Cureton to bring up the right brigade of cavalry, who, in the most gallant manner, dashed in among them and drove them back upon their infantry. Meanwhile a second gallant charge to my right was made by the light cavalry and the body-guard. The Shekawattee brigade was moved well to the right, in support of Brigadier Cureton, when I observed the enemy's encampment and saw it was full of infantry; I immediately brought upon it Brigadier Godby's brigade, by changing front, and taking the enemy's infantry 'en reverse'. They drove them before them, and took some guns without a check.

While these operations were going on upon the right, and the enemy's left flank was thus driven back, I occasionally observed the brigade under Brigadier Wheeler, an officer in whom I have the greatest confidence, charging and carrying guns and everything before it, again connecting his line, and moving on, in a manner which ably displayed the coolness of the Brigadier and the gallantry of his irresistible brigade, – Her Majesty's 50th Foot, the 48th Native Infantry, and the Sirmoor battalion, – although the loss was, I regret to say, severe in the 50th. Upon the left, Brigadier Wilson, with Her Majesty's 53rd and the 30th Native Infantry equalled in celerity and regularity their comrades on the right; and this brigade was opposed to the 'Aieen' troops, called Avitabile's, when the fight was fiercely raging.

The enemy, well driven back on his left and centre, endeavoured to hold his right to cover the passage of the river, and he strongly occupied the village of Bhoondree. I directed a squadron of the 16th Lancers, under Major Smyth and Captain Pearson, to charge a body to the right of the village, which they did in the most gallant and determined style, bearing everything before them, as a squadron under Captain Bere had previously done, going right through a square in the most intrepid manner with the deadly lance. This charge was accompanied by the 3rd Light Cavalry under Major Angelo, and as gallantly sustained. The largest gun upon the field, and seven others, were then captured, while the 53rd Regiment carried the village by bayonet, and the 30th Native Infantry wheeled round to the rear in a most spirited manner. Lieut-Col. Alexander's and Capt Turton's troops of horse artillery under Major Lawrenson, dashed among the flying infantry, committing great havoc, until about 800 or 1000 men rallied under the high bank of a nullah, and opened a heavy but ineffectual fire from below the bank. I immediately directed the 30th Native Infantry to charge them, which they were able to do upon their left flank, while in a line in rear of the village. This native corps nobly obeyed my orders and rushed among the Avitabile troops, driving them from under the bank and exposing them once more to a deadly fire of twelve guns within 300 yards. The destruction was very great, as may be supposed, from guns served as these were. Her Majesty's 53rd Regiment moved forward in support of the 30th Native Infantry, by the right of the village. The battle was won; our troops advancing with the most perfect order to the common focus – the passage of the river. The enemy, completely hemmed in, were flying from our fire, and precipitating themselves in disordered masses into the ford and boats, in the utmost confusion and consternation; our 8-inch howitzers soon began to play upon their boats, when the 'debris' of the Sikh army appeared upon the opposite and high bank of the river flying in every direction, although a sort of line was attempted to countenance their retreat, until *all* our guns commenced a furious cannonade, when they quickly receded. Nine guns were on the river by the ford. It appears as if they had been unlimbered to cover the ford. These being loaded were fired once upon our advance; two others were sticking in the river, one of them we got out; two were seen to sink in the quicksands; two were dragged to the opposite bank and abandoned. These, and the one in the middle of the river, were gallantly spiked by Lieutenant Holmes, of the 11th Irregular Cavalry, and Gunner Scott, of the 1st troop 2nd brigade Horse Artillery, who rode into the stream, and crossed for the purpose, covered by our guns and light infantry.

Thus ended the battle of Aliwal, one of the most glorious victories ever achieved in India, by the united efforts of Her Majesty's and the Honourable Company's troops. *Every gun* the enemy had fell into our hands, as I infer from his never opening one upon us from the opposite bank of the river, which is high and favourable for the purpose – fifty-two guns are now in the Ordnance Park; two sank in the bed of the Sutlej; and two were spiked on the opposite bank; making a total of fifty-six pieces of cannon captured or destroyed.* Many jingalls which were attached to the Avitabile's corps and which aided in the defence of the village of Bhoondree, have also been taken. The whole army of the enemy has been driven headlong over the difficult ford of a broad river; his camp, baggage, stores of ammunition and of grain, – his all, in fact, wrested from him, by the repeated charges of cavalry and infantry, aided by the guns of Alexander, Turton, Lane, Mill, Boileau, and of the Shekawattee brigade, and by the 8-inch howitzers; – our guns literally being constantly ahead of everything. The determined bravery of all was as conspicuous as noble. I am unwont to praise when praise is not merited; and I here most unavowedly express my firm opinion and conviction, that no troops in any battle on record ever behaved more nobly; – British and native, no distinction; cavalry, all vying with H.M.'s 16th Lancers, and striving to head in the repeated charges. Our guns and gunners, officers and men, may be equalled, but cannot be excelled, by any artillery in the world. Throughout the day no hesitation – a bold and intrepid advance; – and thus it is that our loss is comparatively small, though I deeply regret to say, severe. The enemy fought with much resolution: they maintained frequent recontres with our cavalry hand to hand. In one charge, upon infantry, of H.M.'s 16th Lancers, they threw away their muskets and came on with their swords and targets against the lance.

* * *

The fort of Goongrana has, subsequently to the battle, been evacuated, and I yesterday evening blew up the fort of Budhowal. I shall now blow up that of Noorpoor. A position of the

*Eleven guns since ascertained to be sunk in the river, total sixty-seven; thirty-odd jingalls fell into our hands.

peasantry, viz. the Sikhs, appear less friendly to us, while the Mussulmans rejoice in being under our Government.

I have, etc.,

H. G. SMITH,

Major-General Commanding.

Appendix 3

COMMENTS ON THE BATTLE

In a letter from *Colonel Godby*:

'I have no doubt the battle of Aliwal will be esteemed in England as it deserves; it finished a most painful crisis both in India and in England, and its moral effect in Hindostan and the Punjaub was greater than any other achievement of the war. In the Jullundur the natives speak of it as most unaccountable that the soldiers they thought invincible should be overthrown and driven into the river in two or three hours, and be seen scampering through the country before the people had heard of their defeat. The defeat was so clearly and unquestionably done that they ascribed it to supernatural intervention for the many atrocious crimes of the Sikhs, especially upon the oppressed followers of the true Prophet.'

Sir Harry Smith's services at Aliwal were thus acknowledged by *Sir Henry Hardinge*:

'To Major-General Sir Harry Smith, and to the brave troops he commanded, the Governor-General conveys the tribute of his admiration, and the grateful acknowledgements of the Government and the people of India. The service rendered was most important, and was accomplished by the ability of the commander and the valour of the troops.'

Captain Sir John Kincaid, renowned rifleman of the Peninsular, in his generous enthusiasm, wrote a letter signed 'Veteran' to *The Times* of March 30th, to acquaint the public with his friend's past services and military character. Speaking of Peninsular days, he writes: 'Those only who have served under a good and an indifferent staff officer can estimate the immense value of the former, and Smith was one of the very best, for his heart and soul were in his duty. His light wiry frame rendered him insensible to fatigue, and, no matter what battle or march might have occupied the day or night, or what elementary war might be raging, Smith was never to be found off his horse, until he saw every man in his brigade housed, if cover could possibly be had. His devotion to their comforts was repaid by their affection. . . .

No one who knew Harry Smith (his familiar name) in those days could doubt for a moment that whenever he acquired the rank, and the opportunity offered, he would show himself a General worthy of his illustrious preceptor. . . . The battle of Aliwal speaks for itself, as the dispatch of Sir H. Smith would alone proclaim that he had been trained under Sir John Moore and finished under the master-mind of Wellington.'

Sir James Kempt, the revered friend with whom Harry Smith had kept up a monthly correspondence from India, wrote in similar terms:

'You may well be proud, my dear Mrs Sargant, of having such a brother as Harry Smith . . . I have read many details of battles with real pleasure, but I felt something more than pleasure, I felt the highest gratification and delight in reading Harry's admirable dispatch. It is spoken of by every one whom I have seen in terms of the highest praise.'*

The Aliwal dispatch in particular excited unbounded admiration. *Sir Robert Peel* said of it: 'The hand that held the pen used it with the same success with which it wielded the sword.' And *Thackeray's* praise of it in the *Book of Snobs* is a proof that it appealed to a master of literary craft no less powerfully than it appealed to a statesman:

'Let those civilians who sneer at the acquirements of the army read Sir Harry Smith's account of the Battle of Aliwal. A noble deed was never told in nobler language.

'No, no; the men who perform these deeds with such brilliant valour and describe them with such modest manliness, *such* are not snobs. The country admires them, their Sovereign rewards them, and *Punch*, the universal railer, takes off his hat and says, "Heaven save them." '

On the evening of April 2nd the thanks of both Houses were given unanimously by separate resolutions to the victors of Aliwal and Sobraon. In the House of Lords Sir Harry Smith received, to quote *The Times*, an 'unreserved panegyric'† from his worshipped master in warfare, the *Duke of Wellington*. It

*Sir James, writing to Sir Harry Smith himself on 5th April said: 'I well knew that you only wanted an opportunity to display the great military qualities which I knew you possessed in no common degree. . . . Most nobly did you perform your part and show how a battle ought to be fought when the troops are commanded by a skilful and brave General who feels himself "at home" in the thickest of the fight, and who knows how to handle them, and how to make use of each arm at the proper time as an auxiliary to the other. The Great Duke in his speech in the House of Lords makes *you* the Hero of the day. . . . On the day that thanks were voted to you in Parliament, I invited Barnard, Johnny Kincaid, Rowan. Alex. McDonald and other of your old friends and comrades to dine with me, and we drank a bumper to your health and that of Lady Smith.'

†*Professor Sedgwick* wrote similarly: 'I do not believe the old Duke ever spoke so much praise in the course of his life before, and all he said was from the heart.'

cannot be doubted that the proudest moment of Harry Smith's life was that in which he read these words of one so sparing of praise. Some of them were in later days inscribed on his tomb.

'The distant points of the frontier were threatened; Loodiana was threatened – I believe it was even attacked, and the cantonments were burned; and then it was that Sir Harry Smith was sent with a detachment of troops towards Loodiana, taking possession of various points on his road – Durrumkote and other places, of which the enemy had taken possession by bodies of troops which had crossed the Sutlej. And I beg your Lordships to observe that, when Sir Harry Smith was sent, he had three objects in view: one to give security to the post at Loodiana, already reinforced by the arrival there of General Godby after the battle; the others to keep up his communications with the rear by the town of Busseean, a point of great strength and importance, with a view to the communication between Ferozepore and Loodiana, in the front line and Ferozepore and Delhi in the rear, the point from which the heavy train and the means of carrying on the siege in the ultimate operations were to come. These must have passed between twenty and thirty miles of the enemy, while the main body of the army at Ferozepore was not less distant than fifty. These were the objects, to secure which Sir Harry Smith was detached from the army. He marched upon Loodiana, and communicated with the British commander there, who endeavoured to move out to his assistance. While he was engaged with the enemy on this march, which he made in order to perfom a part of his instructions – namely, to maintain the communication with Loodiana, they came out from the entrenched camp and carried off his baggage. I desire to explain that, because it was the only check which the gallant officer met with throughout the whole of this operation, and in fact it is the only misfortune, trifling as it is, which has happened during the whole operations that have taken place in that part of the country. This loss of the baggage, such as it is, has been written up as a great misfortune; but, in point of fact, it could not be otherwise. He was obliged to march within sight of the entrenched camp, from which the enemy had an opportunity of attacking him on his march. I beg your Lordships to observe that Sir Harry Smith had not only to secure his communication with Loodiana, but likewise to secure his junction with General Wheeler, who alone was not able to contend against the enemy. He performed all those objects, was joined by General Wheeler, and then moved on to attack the new position which the enemy had taken up near the river. And, my Lords, I will say upon this, I have read the account of many a battle, but I never read the account of one in which more ability, energy and experience have been manifested than in this. I know of no one in which an officer ever showed himself more capable than this officer has in commanding troops in the field. He brought every description of troops to bear, with all arms in the position in which they were most capable of rendering service; the nicest manoeuvres were performed under the fire of the enemy with the utmost precision, and at the same time with an energy and gallantry on the part of the troops never surpassed on any occasion whatever in any part of the world. I must say of this officer that I never have seen any account which manifests more plainly than he does, that he is an officer capable of rendering the most important services, and of ultimately being an honour to this country.'

In the House of Commons *Sir Robert Peel* moved the vote, with recital of Sir Harry's many services to his country:

'Of the battle itself I will not speak; the victory was complete, and it has been so admirably described by the illustrious commander that I will not weaken the effect of his narrative. And what, let me ask, have been the services of this gallant officer? These recent events have given new lustre to his glory; but he was at the capture of Monte Video – at the attack of Buenos Ayres; he served during the Peninsular War, from the battle of Vimeira to that of Corunna. He was then wounded in another action, but he was at the battles of Sabugal and Fuentes d'Onor and the sieges of Ciudad Rodrigo and Badajos, at the battles of Salamanca, Vittoria, Orthes, the Pyrenees and Toulouse. He was at Washington and at New Orleans, and finally he was at Waterloo. What a series of noble services, and how rejoiced I am that there should be an opportunity, through this new and signal victory, of bringing before the gladdened eyes of a grateful country a long life of military exertion, and an unbroken series of military honours! After he had achieved that success for which we are about to give him our special thanks – after he had driven back the enemy across the Sutlej, he instantly returned to rejoin his commanding officer, Sir Hugh Gough. He arrived on the 8th, two days before the decisive victory gained by the forces under Sir Hugh Gough and Sir Henry Hardinge. But for his services in the victory of the 28th January, I propose that there should be a distinct and separate vote – distinct and separate from that which I shall recommend for that not more glorious, though perhaps more important achievement accomplished at a later date by the whole British army.'

Bibliography

Anon. 1881, *Through the Ranks to a Commission* (1881)

Anon. 1884, *Six Months in the Ranks or The Gentleman Private* (1884)

Anon. 1891, *India Before the Sepoy Mutiny* (1891)

Atteridge, A. H., *The Army* (1906)

Becke, A. F., *Napoleon and Waterloo* (1936)

Blackwood, *Tales from the Outposts* (1933) (II. *Small Wars of the Empire*)

Butler, Sir Wm. F., *Sir Charles Napier* (1890)

Cannon, Richard, *Historical Record of the 53rd Foot* (1838). *Historical Record of the 16th The Queen's Royal Lancers* (1838)

Carey, W. H., *The Good Old Days of Honourable John Company* (1906)

Carman, W. Y., *British Military Uniforms* (1957)

Cole, D. H. and Priestly, E. C., *An Outline of British Military History* (1936)

Collier, Richard, *The Sound of Fury* (1963)

Cork, Barry Joynson, *Rider on a Grey Horse* (1958)

Costello, Edward, *Adventures of a Soldier* (1841)

Cunningham. J. D. (Ed. H. L. D. Garrett), *A History of the Sikhs* (1918)

Cust, R. N., *Pictures of Indian Life* (1881)

De Watteville, H., *The British Soldier* (1954)

Eady, H. G., *Historical Illustrations to Field Service Regulations* (1930)

Edwards, T. J., *Military Customs* (1950)

Field, Cyril, *Old Times Under Arms* (1939)

Forbes, Archibald, *Havelock* (1890). *Colin Campbell, Lord Clyde* (1895). *Memories and Studies of War and Peace* (1895)

Forbes, A., Henty, G. A. and Griffiths, A., *Battles of the 19th Century* (1902)

Fortescue, Sir John W., *A History of the British Army* (1927). *The Last Post* (1934)

Foster, Sir Wm., *John Company* (1906)

Fyler, Colonel, *A History of the 50th or Queen's Own Regiment* (1895)

Gough, Sir Charles and Innes, *The Sikhs and the Sikh War* (1891)
Gough, Sir Hugh, *Old Memories* (1897)
Gowing, T., *A Soldier's Experiences or A Voice From the Ranks* (1906)
Graham, Henry, *History of the Sixteenth, The Queen's, Light Dragoons (Lancers)* (1912)
Grant, James, *British Battles on Land and Sea* (N.D.). *One of the Six Hundred* (N.D.)
Hardinge, Lord, of Penshurst, *Life of Lord Hardinge* (1891)
Hargreaves, Reginald, *This Happy Breed* (1938)
Hay, Ian, *The King's Army* (1938)
Henty, G. A., *Through the Sikh Wars* (1894)
Hohenlohe Ingelfingen, Prince Kraft Zur, *Letters on Cavalry* (1889)
Innes, J. J. McLeod, *Sir Henry Lawrence* (Rulers of India Series) (1898)
Johnson, H. F. H., *British Soldiers*
Kaye, Sir John, *History of the Sepoy War* (1864)
Kipling, Rudyard, *Soldiers Three* (1895). *Barrack Room Ballads* (1892)
Lunt, James, *Charge to Glory* (1962)
MacFarlane, Charles, *History of British India* (1873)
McMunn, Sir George, *Vignettes from Indian Wars* (N.D.). *Behind the Scenes in Many Wars* (N.D.). *Jan Compani Kee Jai* (N.D.)
McMunn, Sir George and Lovett, A. C., *The Armies of India* (1911)
Malleson, G. B., *The Decisive Battles of India* (1888). *The Indian Mutiny of* 1857 (1888)
Marshman, John Clark, *Havelock* (1867)
Moore-Smith, G. C. (Ed.), *The Autobiography of Sir Harry Smith* (1901)
Murray, D. L., *Trumpeter Sound*! (1933)
Newbolt, Sir Henry, *The Thin Red Line* (1931)
Nolan, Dr E. H., *History of the British Empire in India* (1859)
Pearse, Hugh W. and Sloman, H. S., *History of the* 31*st Foot – the East Surrey Regiment* (1898)
Pearson, Hesketh, *The Hero of Delhi* (1939)
Petre, F. Loraine, *History of the Norfolk Regiment* (1905)
Pollock, J. C., *The Way to Glory* (1960)
Pullen, John J., *The Twentieth Maine* (1959)
Rait, Robert S., *The Life and Campaigns of Hugh,* 1*st Viscount Gough* (1903)
Roberts, Lord Fredk., *Forty-One Years in India* (1900)
Robertson, Sir William, *From Private to Field Marshal* (1921)
Sheppard, E. W., *Redcoat* (1952)
Sherer, J. W., *Daily Life During the Indian Mutiny* (1898)
Sleeman, James, *Memoirs of an Indian Official* (1876)

Smith, Vincent, *The Oxford History of India* (1958)
Stocqueler, J. H., *A Personal History of the Horse Guards from 1750 to 1872* (1873). *The Handbook of India* (1844)
Talbot-Booth, E. C., *The British Army, Its History, Customs, Traditions and Uniforms* (N.D.)
Thompson, Edward and Garratt, G. T., *The Rise and Fulfilment of British Rule in India* (1934)
Trotter, L. J., *The Life of John Nicholson* (1897)
Tuker, Sir Francis, *The Chronicle of Private Henry Metcalfe* (1953)
Van Doren Stern, Philip, *Soldier Life* (1961)
Wavell, Field Marshal Earl, *Soldiers and Soldiering* (1953)
Weller, Jac., *Wellington in the Peninsula* (1963)
Whitman, Walt, *Specimen Days* (1882)
Winter, John Strange, *Cavalry Life and Regimental Legends* (1897)
Wolseley, Field Marshal Viscount, *The Story of a Soldier's Life* (1903)
Woodham-Smith, Cecil, *The Reason Why* (1953)
Woodruff, P., *The Men Who Ruled India* (1953). *The Guardians* (1954). *The Founders* (1953)
Wylly, H. C., *Memoirs of Lt-Gen. Sir Joseph Thackwell* (1908)
Wyndham, Horace, *Following the Drum* (1914)
Yonge, C. D., *England's Great Generals* (1893)
Younghusband, G. J., *The Story of the Guides* (1911)
Despatches of the War in India 1846, Lieut.-Gen. Viscount Hardinge, General Lord Gough, Major-Gen. Sir Harry Smith and other sources (1846)
Nominal Rolls of the 16th, The Queen's Lancers. The 53rd Foot. 50th Foot, the Queen's Regiment. 31st Foot, the East Surrey Regiment. 9th Foot, the Norfolk Regiment
October–December 31st 1845 and January–March 31st 1846.
(Public Record Office, London)
The London Gazette
General and Regimental Orders
Letters of Lieut. Bellars (50th Regiment). Lieut. J. D. Robertson (31st Regiment)
Field Service Hygiene Notes – India
The Times
Cornhill Magazine
Illustrated London News
Punch
Army and Navy Gazette
Calcutta Review
Royal Artillery Journal
The Army Quarterly
Soldier Magazine

Blackwoods Magazine
United Services Magazine
The Cavalry Journal
British Model Soldier Society Bulletin
Journal of the Society for Army Historical Research
Parliamentary Reports
Statements and Order Books of Cavalry, Infantry and Artillery
Encyclopaedia Britannica